The
Quandary of Collaboration
with Female School Administrators:
Social Distance in Ghana,
Sub-Saharan Africa

The
Quandary of Collaboration
with Female School Administrators:
Social Distance in Ghana,
Sub-Saharan Africa

Patrick Nicanda Kodzo Allala

iUniverse®

THE QUANDARY OF COLLABORATION WITH FEMALE SCHOOL ADMINISTRATORS: SOCIAL DISTANCE IN GHANA, SUB-SAHARAN AFRICA

iUniverse books may be ordered through booksellers or by contacting:

iUniverse
1663 Liberty Drive
Bloomington, IN 47403
www.iuniverse.com
1-800-Authors (1-800-288-4677)

ISBN: 978-1-4917-5908-0 (sc)
ISBN: 978-1-4917-5909-7 (e)

Print information available on the last page.

iUniverse rev. date: 03/06/2015

CONTENTS

LIST OF TABLES

LIST OF FIGURES

FOREWORD

A characteristic of a potentially important contribution to the literature is when a scholarly work can influence readers to reflect on their personal behaviors and cultural experiences. This book by Dr. Patrick Allala invites the reader to examine his or her belief systems and how they may affect the educational leadership of the country of Ghana.

The psychological literature supports the practice of asking appropriate questions to sensitize individuals to potential biases as well as potential solutions. In the Ghanaian culture, leadership roles have traditionally been ascribed to males. Women have typically been perceived as subordinates. Even though data supports that there are more female teachers than male teachers, very few have held leadership roles such as administrators or headmistresses. However, in the current changing school culture, more women are assuming these roles and it becomes increasingly more important to determine how well they are received, how well they communicate and can lead their school community.

Frequently, personal prejudices and biases are not perceived as such by the individual who holds those views. They are assumed to be statements of fact, not prejudice. In this book Dr. Allala investigates this dynamic by using a technique known as social distance to estimate bias. This methodology, developed and written about by Bogardus (1922-1971), and Triandis (1965-1998) allows one to quantify the degree of social distance, and therefore estimate the level of prejudice through the use of a Social Distance Scale and the Sex Role Egalitarianism Scale. These scales elicit the responses of participants to prompts that which reveals the responders' underlying beliefs. This information can then be used for sensitivity training and mentoring.

Dr. Allala also examined the correlations between the Social Distance and Egalitarianism Scales when looking at age, gender and other social demographical variables, to study the climate in the Ghanaian educational system. Using this methodology, a number of other relevant questions can be asked to investigate other issues of interest. His book presents transparency of the techniques used in terms of their psychometric properties, sampling, research design and statistical analyses.

In my opinion, Dr. Allala's book has great heuristic value in that the suggested methodology opens the door to broader investigations that can improve the educational environment by identifying areas of concern, pointing the way to needed training and providing strategies for effective mentoring. One concern identified through this study is that the "Girl-Child Education" program (GCE) has not yet met its goals, in that the older teachers were identified as being more egalitarian than their younger ounterpoints, thus indicating the possible need for further intervention and research to determine how to improve the GCE program to help it progress towards its intended outcomes. There is additional heuristic value in that Dr. Allala also found significant interactions in the analyses that imply that future research should not be focused at using Main Effect approaches, but should use more sophisticated interactive approaches.

Finally, the Social Distance methodology that Dr. Allala adapted for his research can be widely used in diverse settings, disciplines and countries. It has the potential for framing research questions as they relate to social distance and prejudicial bias. Through this process one may be better able to identify intervention procedures and mentoring strategies.

By: Dr. Isadore Newman, Professor Emeritus.

BRIEF BIO OF
ISADORE NEWMAN, Ph.D.

Dr. Newman is Emeritus Distinguished Professor at The University of Akron, in Ohio where he taught graduate and postgraduate students for 35 years. For the past eight years he has been associated with Florida International University College of Education as a Visiting Director of Graduate Research and Visiting Scholar, as well as an Adjunct Professor. He also holds the title of Adjunct Professor at Andrews University in Michigan where he works with doctoral students and faculty. During his career he has served on over 300 dissertation committees. Dr. Newman is a pioneer in developing and validating novel methodology for multivariate analyses, about which he has authored 17 books and chapters as well as published over 140 refereed articles and he has presented over 300 refereed scholarly papers at national and international conferences. He has been recognized as having published one of the first books and articles introducing mixed methodology and integrated analyses. He also serves on a number of editorial boards and was the primary evaluator on over $10 million in grants.

During his career, Dr. Newman has received many honors, some of which are: the Outstanding Teacher Award for The University of Akron, Outstanding Research Award from The University of Akron, College of Education, Outstanding Evaluator Award from the State of Ohio Department of Mental Health, and Outstanding Reviewer Award from the Educational Researcher, an American Educational Research Association publication, and he held the Distinguished

Harrington Chair in The University of Akron, College of Education. He also was honored with an Outstanding Contribution Award from the AERA Special Interest Group on Multiple Linear Regression, Outstanding Contribution Award from Eastern Educational Research Association, and the Outstanding Alumni Award from Southern Illinois University, College of Education, among others.

Dr. Isadore Newman
Visiting Scholar, College of Education,
Florida International University
Adjunct Professor, Dept. of Human and Molecular Genetics,
College of Medicine, Florida International University
Distinguished Professor Emeritus, The University of Akron

ABSTRACT

In predominantly patriarchal societies, decision-making and authority issues are considered the natural prerogatives of the male figure. Cultures that support such traditional views of gender ideological beliefs tend to ascribe leadership roles to men over their female counterparts. As a result of this, women are perceived as the subordinates in the trade of gender roles and power ascriptions. Women, who defy these culturally held beliefs of male hegemony and thus attain top administrative positions, often struggle in the midst of challenges to establish their authority as superiors. Even though current statistics on teachers show that there are more women than men teachers in the Ghana educational system, only a few of these women hold leadership roles. For example, only a few are administrators or principals.

It is expected that women's occupancy of administrative position within a patriarchal culture will need the test of time and reorientation to become an acceptable norm. Maiden cases will be met with trepidations and cautions. Interactions with these female heads may be difficult and estranged as subordinates struggle to disorient themselves from patriarchal feelings.

Estranged relationships between subordinates and their bosses may affect the degree to which each can contribute to building a good business atmosphere. Consequently, how teachers relate interpersonally with their headmistress can affect the administrative climate of a particular school. The lack of collaboration due to poor interpersonal relationship between teachers and their female principals (i.e., headmistresses) in Ghana can result in ineffective processes of the decision-making apparatus of school administration. It is within this context that the *social distance* prevailing between teachers and their headmistresses is investigated in this study. Knowing what the correlates are and understanding the potentials these relationships have for the administrative climate is crucial for policy implications. Such a study has become more important in the light of the fact that the Ghanaian society is split along two main lineage systems: the patrilineal and matrilineal. These two lineage groups offer different costs and benefits to members, which in turn can affect the social statuses of men and women *vis a vis* how they are perceived and related to in the Ghanaian society. The suggested variables investigated in this study therefore are lineage ties, age, gender, and gender ideological belief (degree of egalitarianism). An examination of the contributions these socio-demographic variables make in determining the social distance between teachers and their headmistresses is of research importance.

Using the Sex Role Egalitarianism Scale (SRES) and the self-constructed Ghana-Specific Behavioral Differential Scale (GSBDS), which have measures on degree of egalitarianism and perceived social distance respectively, I explored the relationship between the predictor variables and social distance of teachers. Findings from the analysis showed that teachers' age and degree of egalitarianism were statistically significant correlates of teachers' perceived social distance towards headmistresses in this Ghanaian sample. These findings lend support to what previous studies have reported from other cultures of the world. However, perceived social distance of teachers towards headmistresses in the Ghanaian second cycle institutions was not a function of teachers' gender and lineage ties.

DEDICATION

This book is dedicated to my parents, Emmanuel Kosi Akondo Allala (of blessed memory) and Perpetua Abra Allala.

ACKNOWLEDGMENTS

I thank the good Lord for His love and providence which guided me all these years to bring a rather long and challenging journey to a successful end. To Him be glory and honor.

I extend my gratitude to Dr. Isadore Newman (Professor Emeritus), a mentor and an inspiration, who was my methodologist at the commencement of my doctoral dissertation. A teacher, whose mentorship enkindled my love, interest and courage for quantitative research and especial for this study. I owe him a debt of gratitude.

May I also express profound gratitude to Drs. Suzanne MacDonald, Kristin Koskey, Bafour Takyi, Huey-Li Li, and Leisa Martin, the five-member committee of my dissertation. Under the able chairmanship of Dr. Suzanne MacDonald, your encouragements, patience, open and constructive comments saw me through many moments of frustration and breaking points. Dr. Kristin Koskey, you broadened my knowledge in statistics and made otherwise challenging moments less problematic. Drs. Bafour Takyi, Huey-Li Li, and Leisa Martin, you will be forever remembered for your frequent emails of encouragement, which in no doubt, pushed me to the finish line. I would be remiss if Dr. Susan Olson is not mentioned here for her ability to help me reorganize and reshape the focus of this study at a time when I almost gave it up due to financial constraints.

I wish to thank the following for their mammoth contributions: Rev. Frs. Paschal Afesi, Major Francis Agble, Raphael Azarias Benuyenah, Jeremiah Ankutsitsia, and Mrs. Victoria Ama Kakabu-Worwornyo, who were my field assistants and all who helped them in the collection of data for this study. May the Good Lord bless you all: Mrs. Ann Holzapfel and

Ms. Jessica McMahon, for helping with the computation of scores and the generation of the data file for statistical analysis; Mr. and Mrs. Bill and Linda Marion for proofreading earlier drafts of the manuscript and Dr. Sesime Adanu for proofreading the final draft of the manuscript.

Finally, but not the least in the line of gratitude, for the prayers and moral support of Rev. Msgr. Wynnand Amewowo, Mr. and Mrs. John and Cartie Antoneli, Dr. and Mrs. Robert and Betty Sobieski, Mr. Mark Raadaway, Mr. John Madia, Rev Dr. Forson Cletus, Dr. Alexander Rock Kofitse, Rev. Fr. Ted Kofitse, Rev. Fr. Ben Adzogba and all who have helped in one way or the other. I share this honor with you with deep gratitude.

CHAPTER I

INTRODUCTION

Background and Statement of the Problem

Collaboration between heads of schools and their teachers is an important constituent for effective school administration (Kise & Russell, 2008). How well accepted a head is by his or her subordinates, determines how willing these subordinates are to associate and/or collaborate with this head for the effective running of their establishment (Amos-Wilson, 1999; Bloom & Erlandson 2003). Hoy and Tarter (1995) maintain that when the authority of the head of a school building, for instance, is either challenged or rejected by subordinates, the ease of participatory administration of that school becomes problematic. Such problems include, but are not limited to, non-cooperation of teachers with principals on decision-making issues, general teacher apathy, and lack of trust among teachers in their principal and the vice versa (Forson, 2007).

A healthy climate of interpersonal relationship (social distance) between teachers and their heads is therefore important for collaborative administration, which is needed for effective running of schools (Forson, 2007). The need for collaborative administration suggests that a good interpersonal climate is prevailing between teachers and their female heads to ensure healthy school administration, *par excellence*. It may be argued here, then, that how comfortable teachers are in their interpersonal relationship with a headmistress has ramifications for the collective output of those teachers themselves, on one hand, and the headmistress, on the other.

School effectiveness may not, therefore, be defined only by collaborative administration but also by the degree and quality of the social distance prevailing between school heads and their teachers. It is the dynamic of such interpersonal relationships that creates the conducive atmosphere that enhances the performance and contribution of all stakeholders within the school building (Kise & Russell, 2008).

In cultures where conventional social barriers favor men as presumed heads over women, female heads may face challenges in altering the strand of boss-acceptance among subordinates. Such a situation may jeopardize the interpersonal relationship between that female head and her subordinates. Understanding the degree of individual teacher's social distance with the female head then is crucial in evaluating school's administrative climate and school outcomes for two reasons: one, because the performance of individual teachers is in pursuit of the educational goal of the building and is guided by the administrative orders of the headmistress, and two, because the acceptance and collaboration with the authority of this female head are salient in achieving the educational goal.

Stereotype-based discrimination and perceived ideologies do determine the extent of interpersonal relationship between people and their out-group (Triandis, 1988). An out-group is defined in this study as any group of people considered to be outside one's own social group (in-group). For instance, men may consider women as their out-group and the vice versa while Blacks may consider Whites as their out-group. Usually, out-groups are considered the inferior or subordinates of the in-group. A person from the out-group is a stimulus person. Studies that have investigated stereotype-based discrimination have concluded that discriminatory attitudes do create greater social distance between the discriminating person and his or her stimulus person (Bogardus, 1971; Triandis, 1988; Wark & Galliher, 2007). In Ghana, some scholars have noted discriminatory attitudes towards female school heads and the rejection of their authority by subordinates (Oduro & MacBeath, 2003). These attitudes could potentially result in socially distancing teachers from their female heads (otherwise referred to in this study as headmistresses) with implications for poor collaborative administration of the building.

Evidence from Ghana and other parts of Africa points to the fact that women heads of schools and other managerial positions are often challenged by status quo hostility in the midst of active patriarchy (Amos-Wilson, 1999; Oduro & MacBeath, 2003; Thakathi & Lemmer, 2002). Amos-Wilson's (1999) study, though it did not directly discuss active discrimination against women, provided support for the need for women to emancipate themselves from culturally supported subordination of women at workplaces. This and other studies maintain that discrimination against female bosses can most effectively be stopped by eschewing beliefs of female subservience. Oduro and MacBeath (2003), for instance, observed that older teachers had the hardest time accepting the authority of the female head of their schools. The younger teachers were found to be more tolerant of the female authority. Consistent with these latter findings, Thakathi and Lemmer (2002) concluded in their study that gender and age, among other variables, are important determinants of the respect or discrimination female heads enjoy or suffer from subordinates. These researchers found that female heads of schools are often discriminated against by virtue of their sex. However, the older they (the female heads of schools) are, the less discriminated against they are among the South African sample of their study.

Cues from these studies led me to postulate that gender ideological belief potentially lends itself as a suspect but prominent factor to be investigated as headmistresses become victims of gender stereotyping. Gender ideological belief is conceptualized as degree of egalitarianism in this study. Egalitarianism is the belief that men and women should be valued as equal entities deserving equal treatment within society; and that no gender group should be considered the subordinate of the other. The opposite of egalitarianism is *traditionalism*, which postulates an imbalance in the treatment of the sexes and sees men as superiors to women, or that women are the subordinates of men. The degree of egalitarianism then is the extent to which a person is willing or not willing to accept egalitarian views. In other words, the degree of egalitarianism is the extent to which one holds the belief that women are as capable as men in given life's situations and can accomplish what men can accomplish and therefore must be accorded the same respect as men have been by society.

In Ghana, of all the studies that have examined discrimination against women supervisors, none has specifically investigated the role played by the degree of egalitarianism in determining the social distance (the level of interpersonal relationship) between these female administrators and their subordinates. A similar observation is made of studies that looked at discrimination against headmistresses by their subordinates (teachers).

In a culture where leadership roles are seen only as men's prerogatives, it is of research importance to examine the conceptual framework within which discrimination toward headmistresses find expression. Understanding the nuances of discrimination against headmistresses is informative for policy implications for a number of reasons: First, to reshape the general orientation of the school community toward collaborative administration of the school. Second, to promote and ensure a professional interpersonal relationship between headmistresses and their subordinates. Third, and to create a climate conducive for effective administration of the school, *inter alia*. The points raised above call for an examination of the perceptions subordinates (teachers) have of their boss (headmistress) and how that perception affects the social distance (interpersonal relationship) between the headmistress and the subordinates. Discriminatory attitude mars efforts of collaboration, breeds resentment, and creates social distance (Bogardus, 1967; Coker, 2005; Triandis, 1965). If school administration depends on the collaborative input of both teachers and heads of buildings (Hoy & Tarter, 1995), then evidence of discrimination against headmistresses in schools must be investigated to determine possible correlates and their effects.

Here, for instance, are some questions that have nurtured my interest for this study:

1. How do teachers in a male dominated (patriarchal) society such as Ghana, in sub-Saharan Africa, view their female supervisors (i.e., how do women and men with less egalitarian gender ideological beliefs perceive their superiors who are women)?
2. Will teachers' perception of their headmistresses determine how they relate to them socially and professionally? In other words, what kind of perceptions do teachers have of the headmistresses

of their schools and what is the degree of teachers' social distance with these headmistresses?

These questions shape the research problem of this study and are relevant in the discussion of issues of policy significance in light of the growing number of females who currently are in school administration in particular (see Table 1). Such questions may evoke responses that shed light on government's attempt to improve the status of women through programs aimed at reducing the gender inequities within the Ghanaian system in general and the educational sector in particular (Allah-Mensah, 2005; Sutherland-Addy, 2002).

In Tables 1, 2, and 3, the distribution of Ghanaians in senior management positions within the public sector is illustrated. Table 1, for instance, demonstrates wide percentage gaps between men and women in the public sector administrations with the men outnumbering the women administrators at an average gap of 86%. For the politically controlled positions, where appointments of leaders are made by government, the percentage of women appears to rise from deputy ministers to ministers, even though not significantly. Twelve percent of the deputy ministers were women, while 15% of the ministers were women, as opposed to 88% and 85% of men, respectively. In the less politically controlled areas, where merit and or system-culture may have played their expected roles, women were abysmally disenfranchised from administrative positions. While only 10% of directors were women, no woman occupied chief director positions. According to Amos-Wilson (1999), this underrepresentation of women is not by chance but rather a characteristic of a cultural idiosyncrasy.

Table 1. *Percentage of Gender Distribution in the Top Four Grades of the Ghanaian Civil Service, 1999*

Grade	Men	Women
Minister	85%	15%
Deputy Minister	88%	12%
Chief Director	100%	0%
Director	90%	10%

Recent studies of the situation revealed no significant changes for the better in the representation of women in managerial positions (see Table 2 and Table 3). Amu (n.d.) averaged 7 years' percentages of women contributing to the economic mainstay of Ghana and found for instance that only 5.8% of Ghanaians in administrative/managerial positions were women. Over 94% of these administrators/managers were men.

Table 2. *Participation of Ghanaian Women in Service Sector*

Sub-sector	%	Count
Wholesale/Retail	55.1	826,340
Hotels/Restaurants	13.4	200,713
Transport/Storage/Communication	3.6	54,214
Financial Intermediation	1.1	16,160
Real Estate/Biz Activity	1.9	28,295
Public Administration	2.0	29,935
Education	6.6	99,107
Health/Social Work	2.4	35,645
Other Community Service	11.2	168,018
Private Households	2.6	38,169
Extra-territorial Organization	0.2	3,169
Total	100	1,500,184

Table 3. *Ghanaian Women's Occupation and Employment (Economically Active Population 7 Years or More)*

Type of Occupation	Count	%
Professional & Technical	340,114	7.6
Admin & Managerial	9,543	0.2
Clerical & Related	83,711	1.9
Sales	906,009	20.2
Agric. Animal & Forestry	2,163,959	48.3
Prod. & Transport Equipment	590,366	13.2
Other	45,821	1.0
Total	4,483,021	100.0

Type of Employment	Count	%
Private Informal	3,816,635	85.1
Semi-public	91,175	2.0
Agric. Animal & Forestry —	—	
NGO/International Organization	29,780	0.7
Other	94,304	2.1
Total	4,483,021	100%

If, indeed, the disenfranchisement and underrepresentation of women in leadership positions are the results of the perception others have of women (Amos-Wilson, 1999; Amu, n.d.), then it may be surmised that women ascendency to leadership positions may incur the aversion of people who hold patriarchal views in the Ghanaian society. Such *patriarchally* oriented persons may distance themselves from the female administrator, thus creating social distance between them and that female head.

If gender discrimination indeed creates social distance between a person and his or her object of discrimination (Bogardus, 1971; Triandis, 1988; Wark & Galliher, 2007), then discrimination towards headmistresses creates social distance between them and their subordinates. Exploring the effect of discrimination on institutional collaboration should guide the educational sector in formulating policies on issues of gender inequity. The formulation of such policies will be better guided if factors underlying discrimination against headmistresses and the effects of that discrimination can be empirically ascertained. For example, such findings would be important aids in *conscientizing* teachers about the need to value headmistresses based on their professional competencies and expertise and not based on any gender stereotypical perceptions.

As noted earlier, of the studies investigating the nuances of gender inequities and attitudes toward headmistresses, in particular, none has empirically looked at socio-demographic variables such as, the degree of egalitarian belief, gender, age, and lineage tie as correlates of social distance with the population of headmistresses. Even though current trends show that the discussion about gender inequities is on-going among Ghanaian scholars (Gedzi, 2009; Minkah-Premo & Dowuona-Hammond, 2005; Minkah-Premo, 2001; Oduro & Macbeath, 2003; Ofori, 2008; Sutherland-Addy, 2002), what seem to be the internal factors determining gender inequalities and inequities, such as people's perceived ideologies, appear to be missed in the gender inequity conversations so far. Filling such a gap with an empirical investigation will be an important contribution to the literature on issues of gender inequities and the disenfranchisement in the Ghanaian second cycle institutions.

Conversations about the construct of social distance, as a function of discriminatory attitudes have featured mainly in the socio-psych literature. Social distance is defined here as the social interpersonal gap created between two people or groups of people as a result of some perceived ideological beliefs (Triandis, 1988). In educational administration, this concept of social distance is new and yet very important in understanding certain phenomena of the organizational dynamics vis-à-vis stakeholders' interpersonal relations. Explaining this dynamic sociologically may help our understanding of the practical ramifications of any relationship between egalitarian belief and social distance among actors.

Theoretical Perspectives of the Study

Many theories have been proposed by social scientists to explain human attitudes and interpersonal relationships in given situations. Such theories attempt to offer the conceptual framework within which people's behavior may be explained and also give reasons to why people behave the way they do. Prominent among these theories are *symbolic interactionism* and the *embedded group theories*. Functionally, these theories have been employed sometimes to explain the trade of relationships within family circles (Boss, 1993; Rosenblatt & Fisscher, 1993), behavior patterns within organizational setups (Beale, 1980) and the dynamics of interaction between superiors and subordinates (McConnell, 1993).

Conceptually, these two theories lend themselves to pervasive cultural indices such as shared norms and values, myths, and stories, rituals and ceremonial events, which do influence people's behavior and, even so, do construct the kind of identity genre by which individuals are known and by which they act and relate in society (Roberts & Hunt, 1991). Belief-systems and the meaning human beings attach to things, therefore, affect the way they interact and react to persons and situations. Within the contexts of such theoretical frameworks, it can be argued, for instance, that gender discrimination exists because people attach a certain meaning to what it is to be a man or a woman in society, based on their beliefs about particular normative gender statuses and role expectations of the sexes by their cultures.

Coined in 1937 by Herbert Blumer, and later expanded by several scholars, symbolic interactionism postulates that the attitudes and behavior of human beings towards things are the direct functions of the meanings they have for these things (Lynch & McConatha, 2006; Rosenbaum, 2009). Conceptually then, a person's attitude towards the one he or she perceives as poor and wretched, for instance, will be different from his/her attitude towards the person he/she perceives as wealthy and honorable. For example, the one considered to be rich and honorable may be very well respected and treated with honor in society while the person considered to be poor and socially insignificant may go without being noticed and may, sometimes, be ignored by the same group that honored the rich.

In much the same way, the kind of treatment the one perceived as a superior receives from an individual may very much be at variance with that which a subordinate receives from that same individual. Consequently, behavior patterns may change from persons to persons depending on the actors' perceptions of his/her objects of interaction. We can infer from these theoretical assumptions then, that it is possible to predict human behavior in given situations if the domain (object) of that interaction is known.

Embedded group theorists like Alderfer and Smith (1982), for instance, opine that relationships between people are embedded in a network of affiliations that include both personal identity group (e.g., ethnicity, age and gender), and task groups such as organizational levels and professional specializations. This theory argues that human beings have myriads of identities whose meaning must be understood in the context of the organizational and/or societal history of interaction of the identity groups.

Gender discrimination, as a culturally held norm, finds notable expression within the context of these theoretical definitions. In a patriarchal society, for instance, it is generally understood that men occupy leadership roles by virtue of their gender. Authority and decision-making privileges therefor remain a man's prerogatives. As a result of this male leverage, a female administrator and decision-maker in a patriarchal society, with male subordinates, may be viewed as a social nuisance, a challenge to the normative masculine hegemony, a move to over-stepping feminine boundaries, and a threat to male authority. Potentially, such internal conflicts, with gender stereotypical dispositions as their undercurrents, could lead to the existence of a greater degree of social distance between teachers and their female heads. In effect, such consternations may evoke socio-psychological power conflicts, thus, creating relationship problems that may jeopardize the prospects of successful running of that institution. In a school environment, therefore, such a conflict comes with its negative ramifications for administrative performance of teachers and heads of that institution (Cox & Nkomo, 1993; Shum & Cheng, 1997).

The Sociocultural Setting in Ghana

The difficulty here lies in the traditional notion that women are inferior to men; hence, any exercise of authority, expressed in administrative orders from the female superior, constitutes a threat to men's traditionally and culturally inherited superiority complex (Gueye, 2010). The leadership position of a headmistress may be viewed as a challenge to male hegemony and may even constitute an act of intimidation; it may also be viewed as a potential revolt against an enduring traditional norm of patriarchy (Skrla, Reyes, & Scheurich, 2000). The assumption derived from these theories is that any subordinate (male or female) with such traditional feelings and *felt urges* would relate to that female supervisor/superior with attitudes connoting a discriminatory type.

Prejudices that beget discrimination potentially lead to negative interaction between different subgroups (Coker, 2005). Between a supervisor and a subordinate in a work environment, discriminatory attitude is not a healthy professional constituent and may not promote effective management of the institution. Dispositional factors, then, become salient in the discussion of teachers' perception of and relationship with a female-headed administration in a society that is significantly alive with patriarchal orientations.

Ghana is not only a patriarchal society but also has two major lineage systems that view the statuses of men and women differently. These lineage systems (patrilineal and matrilineal ties) determine the inheritance prerogatives of individual members within their respective lineage blocs. Since inheritance determines the ontological value of a societal member within the Ghanaian community, lineage ties are serious legacies.

In the patrilineally organized societies, descent of family members and inheritance prerogatives are traced from the male pedigree. Prominently, positions of headship and decision-making in the family are the prerogatives of the man's. This culturally accorded social status men enjoy makes them very important social figures, especially in the patrilineal cultures of Ghana, a sub-Saharan African country (Nukunya, 1987; Osmond & Thorne, 1993; Sugarman & Frankel, 1987). In the Akan matrilineal system of Ghana, however, lineage and inheritance rights are traced along maternal lines, making mothers, and for that matter, all women, very important figures in the Akan society. Even though matrilineal women do not directly have ownership rights, their children trace ownership rights through them and inherit properties of their mothers' brothers (Takyi & Broughton, 2006; Takyi & Gyimah, 2007). According to Takyi and

Gyimah (2007), children from matrilineal systems traditionally do not have ownership rights along paternal lines. In other words, they cannot inherit their father's property; that belongs to their father's nephews from their father's sister. In a duo-lineage society like Ghana with such twists, gender roles and status ascription for men and women become very complex and yet important; not only to the sexes, but also for the understanding of society's response to such social arrangements. These two elements (gender roles and status ascriptions) are salient in determining the rights enjoyed by individual members. They shape and emphasize how men and women are perceived and treated in the Ghanaian society (Nukunya, 1987).

Noteworthy is that even among the matrilineal Akan group, the right of inheritance (which is usually along the mother's line) has never been confused with the roles men play as heads of the household. As observed by Takyi and Broughton (2006), men in the Ghanaian society have always occupied leadership positions in the family setting, irrespective of their lineage ties. As a social organization then, the patriarchal system creates a culture of male hegemony and female subordination regardless of lineage prerogatives. In an enduring manner then, this patriarchal ideology is salient in shaping male-female relationship with an understanding of the kind of social status it ascribes to both sexes (Nukunya, 1987; Sugarman & Frankel, 1996; Takyi & Gyimah, 2007).

Even when empowered by higher academic achievement and socioeconomic privileges, women's consciousness about their boundaries on decision-making prerogatives easily defers to men. Indeed, Takyi and Gyimah (2007) maintained that even in the matrilineal society, where women enjoy some intra-clan prominence, when it comes to inheritance prerogative, decision-making is often always a male franchise. According to scholars, the reason for this is simple; men are traditionally held as the superordinates of the society (Amos-Wilson, 1999; Kannae, 1993; Takyi & Broughton, 2006). We may ask these questions then that in such a culture, will it become a clash of norms to have women in leadership positions, assume decision-maker roles, with men among their subordinates? Will gender discrimination *vis-à-vis* gender role expectations play any role here? How well accepted will a headmistress be by her teachers? Will alienation of the headmistress by her subordinates be the corollary of such cultural arrangements within the Ghanaian context? So far, there is a void in the available literature on gender issues in Ghana addressing these questions. Further, whether or not the importunate issues of discrimination against women are a function of the enduring gender ideological beliefs of societal members has not yet been explored in the literature.

Given these observations, an investigation into the relevancy of the social functions these lineage patterns play in teachers' behavioral dispositions toward headmistresses may reveal interesting findings unique to the social distance construct. In Ghana, the patrilineal group is comprised mainly of the Ewes, Gas, Guans and most of the Northern tribes. The matrilineal society is comprised of mainly the Asantes, Fantes, and Nzimas, all of which are referred to as Akan societies (Nukunya, 1987; Takyi & Gyimah, 2007). These divisions, as stated above, are based on the differentials in rights of inheritance and the ascription of social status enjoyed by lineage members often traced along either of the parental genders.

Study Purposes

The purpose of this exploratory study, therefore, is to examine the relationship between the degree of egalitarianism, lineage ties, gender, and age of teachers from second cycle institutions in Ghana and teachers' self-reported degree of social distance with headmistresses. Egalitarianism is defined in this study as teachers' unbiased views and attitude towards their headmistress regardless of her sex. Teachers who express non-biased gender views of their headmistress therefore hold that the sex of their headmistress should not influence how they perceive her in her role as a leader. Such egalitarian beliefs should acknowledge her (equal) rights, potentials, abilities, and authority as a leader in much the same way as will be accorded a male counterpart. Accordingly, she should not be assessed based on her sex but, rather, valued for what she is capable of as a leader.

The degree of egalitarianism was measured by the Sex-Role Egalitarianism Scale (SRES). Lineage affiliation is defined as teachers' belongingness to either the patrilineal or the matrilineal descent of the Ghanaian society as stated by the respondents. This definition of lineage ties draws from Bohmig's (2010) and Takyi and Broughton's (2006) assertions that lineage ties determine one's inheritance prerogatives, thereby increasing one's autonomy and social value in the Ghanaian society. Age and gender of teachers will be as indicated by the teachers. Social distance as measured by the Ghana-Specific Behavioral Differential Scale (GSBDS) is the interpersonal closeness a teacher is willing to have with his or her headmistress (see GSBDS in Appendix A). In other words, it involves how willing a teacher is to associate or interact on a personal level with the female head of his or her school.

Significance of the Study

This study takes a sociological view of the dynamics of social interaction between the two most important groups of stakeholders in school building administration. It evaluates the importance of interpersonal relationship between teachers and heads of school buildings for effective administrative collaboration. By examining the degree of self-reported social distance between teachers' and their female heads, this researcher seeks to initiate discussion about the discrimination against women heads of schools and the potential debilitating ramifications that this could have on effectiveness of school management in Ghana. The rejection of a school administrator's authority may be due to the personal or collective views of teachers about that administrator. When teachers' views about their head make them doubt his or her ability to be head, or when those views make teachers question the administrative deftness of that head, then there is the potential for the lack of collaboration with that head.

The lack of participatory or cooperative administration could lead to poor outcomes for organizational effectiveness (Lee, 2001). In a school environment, discrimination against a headmistress could affect not only the functioning of the female headmistress, but also on the performance of teachers whose attitudes towards the relationship with the female headmistress become affected by the gender ideological beliefs they hold. The implications of this for students, who are at the receiving end of the educational equation, are damaging.

The paucity of literature exposing this problem raises concerns, especially as Ghana continues to pursue its Girl-Child Education Initiative launched in 1994. As evident from Tables 1, 2, and 3, and later in Table 4, there have been no significant outcomes after a decade of its inception. With figures that give too little for any hope in the future, investigations into why the problem still exists are imperative to inform policy. The fact that none of the previous studies investigated the contribution of the degree of egalitarian beliefs on the disenfranchisement of women in Ghana makes this current study even more crucial.

Equally important, new research activities are needed that look at the nuances of gender discrimination, especially regarding people's social distance with female managers, which have not received such research attention. This study then contributes in filling that gap. The awareness and conscientization this brings to teachers is that administrators should be valued for their competencies and expertise and should not be judged by the fact of their sex. The purpose of this study, therefore, is to explore the issues of gender discrimination and how that impacts teachers' social distance with their headmistress. Such an investigation will also help in clarifying assumptions about people's social distance with their female administrators, whether in the educational sector or outside it.

Delimitations

The scope of this study was limited to the investigation of the relationship existing between degree of egalitarianism of Ghanaian teachers in secondary schools headed by headmistresses and teachers' social distance with these headmistresses. The gender ideological belief being measured here pertains only to the degree of egalitarianism. It does not involve a measure of traditional gender ideology or traditionalism even though a less egalitarian person is more likely traditional than egalitarian. Other predictor variables of the study include lineage ties, gender, and age of teachers. The criterion variable is teachers' perceived social distance with their headmistresses.

It is possible that there are better predictors of teachers' social distance than the variables employed by this study. However, this study limits its investigations exclusively to the predictor variables mentioned above.

Operational Definition of Terms

Age. The self-reported ages of teachers and will be indicated by teachers' self-reported ages in years.

Egalitarian gender ideology or egalitarianism. The individual's view of men and women as equally endowed with potentials that put both sexes on the same social platform without any discrimination (King & King, 1993). Hence it is the belief that whatever men are capable of accomplishing women, too, are capable of achieving; and that no sex is superior to the other. For this study, egalitarianism refers to a gender ideological belief that perceives headmistresses of second cycle institutions in Ghana as equally capable and efficient as their male counterparts. In other words, equity and equality should guide the trade of power and authority between men and women. The degree to which respondents are egalitarian will be determined by the SRES scale.

Gender. This is the self-reported sex of individual teachers on the demographic section of the questionnaires as to whether they are male or female.

Gender ideological belief. The belief system upheld by the individual that makes him/her think that there are gender specific roles for men as there are for women which define their statuses in society and the social roles they are expected to play (Koivunen, Rothaupt, & Wolfgram, 2009).

Matrilineal affiliation. The individual teacher's belongingness to the ethnic group that traces inheritance along the lineage of the mother. This will be indicated by the respondent on the demographic section of the GSBDS survey instrument.

Patriarchal ideology. The individual's support for the traditional belief that men are the stronger, the authority figure, the head, the decision-maker, or the superior figure to women who must be considered the less capable, subservient, inferior to males and subordinates of them (Kambarami, 2006; Lorier, 2008; Minkah-Premo & Dowuona-Hammond, 2005; Ofei-Aboagye, 1994). Teachers with beliefs in male hegemony have the patriarchal view of society and will express less egalitarian views as measured by the SRES.

Patrilineal. The belongingness of the individual teacher to the ethnic group that traces inheritance along paternal descent. This will be indicated by the respondent on the demographic section of the GSBDS survey instrument.

Social distance. The degrees of closeness or acceptance an individual reports feeling toward a person of his/her out-group (Bogardus, 1947). In other words, social distance is the perceived degree of the gap of interpersonal relationship between individuals and their stimulus persons. In this study, social distance is defined as the affective distance resulting from teachers' willingness or non-willingness to associate with their headmistresses in the Ghanaian second cycle institutions. Degree of social distance is the dependent variable of the study and will be measured by the GSBDS.

Summary

Chapter I began by identifying the problem of the study and gave rationale for the investigation of this research problem and laid out which factors need to be tested specifically. The evidence of social distance or the degree of interpersonal relationship between teachers and their headmistresses could be an obvious index of the disposition for collaboration or the lack of it. When teachers' perceived gender ideological beliefs lead them to contract strong social ties with their headmistresses (Loder, 2005), there is potential for collaborative administration of the school building with positive outcomes for school effectiveness (Forson, 2007).

The non-willingness to associate with and the rejection of a headmistresses' authority by teachers, simply because of her sex, will create social distance between teachers and their female heads (Loder, 2005; Tang, 2004).

In this opening chapter the degree of egalitarianism, lineage ties, gender and age, were identified as potential determinants of teachers' social distance with headmistresses of second cycle academic institutions in Ghana. In the gender stratified Ghanaian society, the male dominance ideology plays very significant roles in determining the quality of interaction between men and women (Amos-Wilson, 1999). Researchers who have investigated attitudes toward female school heads in Ghana maintained that there is the presence of gender discrimination against these headmistresses (Oduro & MacBeath, 2003).

It is observed in some of these studies that older teachers, compared to the younger teachers, are the more opposing of their headmistresses' authority. Such discriminatory attitudes have the potentials of making interpersonal relationships between teachers and their headmistresses problematic. The lack of interpersonal relationship between teachers and their headmistresses is the presence of social distance between these teachers and the headmistresses of their schools. The objective of this research investigation is to determine whether the degree of egalitarianism, lineage affiliation, gender, and age are the functions of teachers' perceived social distance with their headmistresses.

CHAPTER II

LITERATURE REVIEW

A major preliminary problem encountered in doing this study is the paucity of data-supported socio-demographic literature in the field of education in Ghana. For instance, a personal visit in 2005 to the Headquarters of the Ministry of Education, Ministries, Accra, in search of data on the gender distribution of heads of second cycle institutions in Ghana yielded no utilitarian result. The only data information available was a document entitled *Ghana Education Service, Secondary Education Division: Addresses of Secondary Schools 2004/2005,* which only contained information on institutional addresses and whether an institution was unisex or co-educational. There were no data on which of the 476 second-cycle institutions had a male head or female head; or how many men to women were teachers at these schools. A similar attempt was made in 2010 (five years later) for data request and the result was the same. The second cycle division of Ghana education service could not produce data on gender ratio of heads of institutions. In the academia also, there were no specific studies on social distance between teachers and their female heads nor have previous scholars investigated such a phenomenon between subordinates and their female bosses within the general Ghanaian work environment.

This chapter is composed of two sections. The first section is a composite of ancillary literature, drawing evidence from the Ghanaian socio-cultural milieu that supports the investigator's claim of a culturally supported discrimination and disenfranchisement of women in Ghana. The second section reviewed literature on the general perceptions of the women population as a result of the culturally supported idiosyncrasy of male hegemony and female subordination evidenced in the Ghanaian society. The interplay of all of these in determining social distance between teachers and their headmistresses is conclusive with buttressing evidence from other world cultures.

The Ghanaian Sociocultural Background

To better understand the gender situation in Ghana and women's struggle to acquire leverage and respect for their authority as leaders, a review of some of the socio-cultural disadvantages for the Ghanaian woman is *sine qua non*. It has been mentioned earlier that the Ghanaian society is predominantly patriarchal—upholding views of culturally supported male hegemony and female subordination. Gender roles and intra-gender relationships are not based on biological differences between men and women; they are the direct determinations of the socio-cultural beliefs shaped by the traditions of the people and preserved by societal norms (Ardayfio-Schandorf, 2005; Tanye, 2008). In the highly gender stratified Ghanaian society, therefore, the male dominance ideology plays very significant roles in determining the quality of relationship that exists between men-women. This socio-culturally guided perception of gender role expectations in the Ghanaian society, much like any patriarchal society, turns to favor the men over their female counterparts (Runger, 2006). The motivations people receive for academic mobility is pervasively gender biased. As more men than females receive higher education, opportunities of leadership positions fall naturally in men's favor.

The Fate of the Ghanaian Woman

Before the launching of the campaign for the girl-child education, there was not any national consciousness and the exigencies for girls to pursue higher education with equal emphasis as it is for their male counterparts (Sossou, 2006). Evidence from previous studies indicated that majority of women who are academically inclined and have the support of their families to pursue higher education, do so to the secondary school level only and then give it up (Sutherland-Addy, 2002). Some of these girls drop out only when they are at the threshold of tertiary education. Findings from some qualitative studies revealed that factors contributing to this phenomenon include, but are not limited to, the apprehension on the part of women that they will become unmarriageable after their scholarly attainments since prospective men avoid highly educated women for wives. Another huddle for the women is the general view of families (sponsors), that girls (women) do not need higher education to serve society (Sossou, 2006; Stephens, 2000), hence should not aspire for higher academic goals.

For example, Sossou, (2006) observed that highly educated women often end up being shunned by prospective husbands probably for fear (on the part of men), that with their education, wives might vie for power and authority with them, which will make them (wives) difficult to control and subverted. Since mothering is one of the cherished social roles for the Ghanaian woman, education, which appears to remove women from statutory motherhood, is not often encouraged for the girl-child (Sossou, 2006; Sutherland-Addy, 2002). In these circumstances, many women turn to follow educational programs that offer professional skills in the short term so as to allow them the opportunities of childbearing and mothering. Training for careers such as clerical and secretarial jobs, therefore, become the preferred educational track options for most women who mold themselves into secretaries, account clerks, typists, library assistants, tellers at the bank, among others. The few who outlie the status quo and excel men into placements as managers and administrators have to fight the systemic barriers to attain these superior statuses otherwise acknowledged as male-type positions. These women stand the risk of being discriminated against (Tanye, 2008).

Some scholars (e.g., Ardayfio-Schandorf, 2005; Gedzi, 2009) maintained that, to a great extent, society's unfair role-expectation of Ghanaian women puts them at the beck and call of their husbands or of their male counterparts and reduces their roles to mere aides in the society. Thus, these studies maintained that tensions and conflicts are the inevitable consequences of a woman's failure to observe this traditionally held norm of male-superiority and female-subordination. Even though such assertions sound too strong to be believed, one cannot dismiss them entirely. They all share characteristics of possible vestiges of enduring patriarchy of the Ghanaian type.

Violence Against Women

A study by a North American based Ghanaian attorney, Ofei-Aboagye (1994), was one of the few early scientific works on violence against women in Ghana. This study had a dyadic approach to the issue of discrimination against women. The first section investigated the incidence of domestic violence against women, and the second approach examined the contributions made by some aspects of the Ghanaian traditional culture in perpetuating and supporting this gender biased aggression. The concern here was to establish a correlation between the two, if any existed. Consequently, Ofei-Aboagye administered questionnaires to clients of the Legal Aid Clinic of the International Federation of Female Lawyers (FIDA) between May 1991 and August 1991.

Only 50 out of the over 200 women with domestic violence related problems agreed to answer the questionnaires for fear of the unknown implications of what their testimonies might bring upon them. According to Ofei-Aboagye (1994), the reason is simple: Ghanaian women are discouraged from sharing evidence of their domestic problems with strangers probably just so to avoid the punishment that might follow from their husbands for not disciplining their tongue (see also Amoakohene, 2004; Ardyfio-Schandorf, 2005). Measuring the acceptance of male superiority and female domination, using the second version of questionnaires, the study found that almost all the women agreed that beating as a kind of disciplinary act is the prerogative of men. Thus, the researcher concluded that wife battering was prevalent and accepted in the Ghanaian society even by some women.

Only 2 out of the 50 participants said beating of any kind transcends the norm. Some of the reasons given by the women as causes for their beating included: "When I confronted him with evidence of his adultery," "When I asked for chop money" (in Ghana housekeeping money is called chop money), "When I refused to have sex with him," "He said I was rude in public," "Because my cooking was not to his taste," "I had insulted his mother," and "I spent too much money." The above study revealed clear dominance of men over women and speaks also to the general acceptance of male dominance by the society.

The issue of male dominance over women, according to Sossou (2006), transcends the scattered incidences of abusive relationships and male violence against women. It is idiosyncratic and rooted in the mode of the cultural socialization of the people. Sossou maintains that it is not men alone who believe in their hegemony but also some women accept the traditional gender ideology of male-power over women. Power ascriptions and decision making in such a society, therefore, is naturally deferred to men, leaving women at the base-level positions, whether in the formal or informal sectors of the politico-socio-cultural lives of the people.

To crystallize our discussion about the issues of discrimination against women in the Ghanaian society, it is important to examine some of the key socio-political-cultural institutions of that society such as: cultural practices, formal education, formal sector and political life, and the management of schools itself.

Discriminatory Cultural Practices

The rich culture of Ghana may be admired for its kaleidoscopes of positive elements such as the warm hospitality towards strangers, the value of family, courteous pleasantries towards others (regardless of age and social standing), respect for human life, and the pursuit of peace, among others. Nonetheless, some Ghanaian traditions and religio-cultural practices undermine the import of this cultural richness as they attack the dignity of women and jeopardize their place in society (Agboka, 2006; Selby, 2008). These traditional and religio-cultural beliefs and practices set the parameters for women's legacy and natural rights and curtail their social prerogatives and privileges in the midst of active patriarchy. The male privileged culture gives men (young and old) the first place in society over women.

According to Tanye (2008), it is a cultural expectation that Ghanaian women in the family are supposed to look up to the male figures of their household for protection and the provision of needs in much the same way as minors of the household do. As observed earlier, men are socialized to assume caretaker authority roles over women, be they their sisters, wives or mothers, and are expected to execute sanctions on their female counterparts when they gaffe (Minkah-Premo & Dowuona-Hammond, 2005). Even cultural practices, meant for the observance of all, treat the sexes differently; they do not take kindly to women when it comes to enforcing their observances. They always favor men and neglect the interest of women (The Women's Manifesto for Ghana, 2004). A discussion of some of these practices and held norms is next.

Extraneous widowhood rite. Widowhood rite is common to all tribes among the Ghanaian society after the death of one's spouse (Agboka, 2006; Selby, 2008). Widowhood rites depict the ritual mourning period observed by the surviving spouse to show the depth of grief, love, and commitment to the deceased (on the part of the surviving spouse) even after his/her death. Both widowers and widows observe the widowhood rite. However, among some of the Ghanaian tribes, women are often subjected to more rigorous and dehumanizing observances that may even be harmful to their mental and physical health (Agboka, 2006; Selby, 2008; The Women's Manifesto for Ghana, 2004).

In some tribes, while men have the option of a 6-month period of observance, women are often subjected to a full year of widowhood rite. Dehumanizing practices such as passing the first three nights of the one-year period in the kitchen, shaving of the head, and making occasional midnight trips to the riverside alone. An interview with a widow from the Gbi traditional area of mid-eastern Ewes of Ghana revealed that their widows wear tattered clothes, shave their heads every fortnight, walk through the forest in the middle of the night alone to the riverside for ritual bath in a stream (three times during the 1-year period), talk always in whispers (never raising their voices to talk to others), desist from all commercial undertakings, cannot eat late in the night, and wear dark clothing throughout the entire 1-year widowhood period spinning cotton into treads. These are requirements for women only (Worwornyo, October 15, 2008). Men also wear dark clothes but do not observe the other restrictions and do not have to spin cotton. The fact that women go through such odious extremes while men have the option of less rigorous observances is an index of disfavor against women and contains an element of discrimination which defines women's social status.

Inheritance and male-biased land tenure system. Customary laws of inheritance differ from tribe to tribe and from one lineage system to another (Gedzi, 2009). According to the Ghana Living Standards Survey (GLSS, 2008), Ghana, a Third World country and one of the poverty-stricken sub-Saharan countries, has an average unemployment rate of 3.6%. Even though this percentage rate is the same for both genders, the urban centers averagely report higher percentages of 6.3% with Accra, the capital of Ghana, recording 8.9% than the rural settings of 1.6% (GLSS, 2008). In a country where about 70% of its citizens depend on the yield of the land to survive, ownership of land and the tenure system that determines how land is acquired, become crucially important. Land ownership in Ghana is mainly acquired through lineage inheritance. However, it is not customary for women to own family land through inheritance (Gedzi, 2009; Runger, 2006).

Family land is shared among the male siblings while female siblings are allowed to work on the land only as temporary owners until they are married away. Married women work on their husbands' land for as long as they remain married to them and often lose the land during divorce or death of their husbands (Aryeetey, 2002; Tsikata, 1997). The cultural assumption is that women/wives as well as children of the marriage only assist the man (husband and father) in acquiring his wealth whether on the farm or in the business (Aryeetey, 2002). They are never co-owners of the land or business. As noted by scholars, the woman, especially, is just a temporary beneficiary of the man's property for as long as the marriage existed (Peters, 2010; Quisumbing, Payongayong, Aidoo, & Otsuka, 1999; Whitehead & Tsikata, 2003). She does not have equal rights as the man to properties acquired during the marriage.

The fact being emphasized by the above studies is that, even though traditional regulatory observances exist about male-head custodianship of land, there is no written contract on them, no written provisions, and their terms are unknown; and yet they have the force of law purely based on customary assumptions strictly adhere to by the people. The lineage head (always a man) is the custodian of the family land. It is he who distributes land among members of the family. His role as custodian of the lineage land comes with the power and authority to assign and unassign land ownership to whomever it must be assigned (Gedzi, 2009; Ofori, 2008). That this *bona fide* custodianship is never a woman's office nor is it a female prerogative, speaks volumes of how women are perceived in the Ghanaian culture. It should be noted that even in the matrilineal system, where inheritance is traced along mother's line, one can only inherit the property of mother's male relatives (such as maternal uncles) and not mother's own property since women do not typically own family properties (Nukunya, 1992; Takyi, 2007).

What is of concern here is not how the women lose the land, but why they do not have ownership rights as their male counterparts, and why customary laws preclude them from owning land on which everyone's livelihood depends? The most plausible explanation for this culturally supported ownership imbalance is the perception the Ghanaian society has of women as the less valued gender species. Another way to interpret customary expectation is that: they (women) should not have equal rights with men; they should be seen as a lower order group that comes second to the male group; and that they should have no voice when it comes to ownership rights, power and authority privileges. In a culture where societal members share such perceptions, the ascendancy of women to authority and leadership positions will be an out-of-the-ordinary occurrence and may be resented by the people. This trade of inequality and inequity of rights and privileges between the sexes clearly emphasizes isolation and discrimination against women within this sub-Saharan African culture.

Even though recent governments have attempted to address this issue by promoting women's right (the 1992 Republican Constitution and The Intestate Succession Law), the force and legitimacy of the customary laws and traditions have undermined and often render such government attempts ineffective. Evidence from the Ghanaian culture can verily then be contextualized in this assertion of Lind, and Huo (2000) that, "… general cultural values influence individuals' attitudes and behaviors within particular social situations" (p. 1139). It will, therefore, not be overrated to propose that this general attitude towards women in the Ghanaian sub-Saharan society is a function of an ideological belief that undermines the status of women as equal competitors with their male counterparts.

Trokosi. The name *Trokosi* means slave of the gods. Family members sacrifice a virgin from the family to appease the gods for the crime(s) of a family member, who may long be dead. According to scholars, the people believe that failure to pay the fine may bring calamities upon them by the gods. Once in the shrine these girls (considered as slaves of the gods) become sex objects for the shrine priests. They are not allowed to attend school or learn any trade; they are forbidden from receiving any healthcare needs and proscribed from mingling with the general public without supervision (Aird, 2010; Ben-Ari, 2001).

In my judgment one of the noted most dehumanizing religious practices of the African traditional religion in Ghana is the *Trokosi* cult. This cult violates the most fundamental human rights of females, robbing them young of their womanhood and the potential of their usefulness to society (see also Aird, 2010; Ameh, 1998; Owusu-Ansah, 2003; Tanye, 2008). That these virgins become sex-slaves for the priest of the shrine, there is no humanly imaginable justification for the *Trokosi* cult. The practice of the enslavement of female virgins into shrines of the fetish priests as fines paid to the shrine for crimes committed by a family member or by some ancestor of the family is simply horrible, barbaric and dehumanizing. *Trokosi* is nothing but cruelty and unfair victimization of the female group. According to Aird (2010), the *Trokosi* cult is found among the Torgnu of southern Ewe in the Volta Region, the Ga-Adangmes of Greater-Accra region of Ghana, Togo, Benin, and the southwestern part of Nigeria. *Trokosi* is still the practice among some of the coastal tribes of Sub Saharan Africa today (Ameh, 1998; Ben-Ari, 2001; Owusu-Ansah, 2003; Tanye, 2008). It is believed that the practice of *Trokosi* has been around for over 300 years now.

Most of these sex slaves were taken in their prime of teenage life and some others as young as toddlers (Aird, 2010). These shrine sex slaves are literally at the beck and call of the shrine priest solely for the satisfaction of his sexual whims. It is the priest of the shrine who determines the number of years a *Trokosi* (the slave of the gods), is expected to serve in the shrine. They are then allowed their freedom if their families can pay the fine imposed by the fetish priest. However, the fine imposed for the purchase of the freedom of the *Trokosis* is often beyond the economic solvency of their families, hence making a temporary enslavement in the shrine a perpetual ordeal for these *Trokosis* (Aird, 2010; Ben-Ari, 2001; Lorier, 2008). This blatant exploitation and heinous abuse of these damsels, who could otherwise become productive citizens of their communities, do limit their utility in society and remove them from competing with their male counterparts academically thus robbing them of their future leadership opportunities.

The question this researcher is compelled then to ask here is, why is it that only females are used as fines to appease the gods and not also young males? If servitude in the shrines by a young blood of the family of an offending member or ancestor suffices to appease the gods, then the gender of the slave should not matter. That young females become the coveted prices imposed by these *Trokosi* shrines and not also young males, emphasizes how that culture perceives the right and dignity of women, whose abuse is urged by the whims and caprice of the traditions of the people. It is the conclusion of this researcher that *Trokosi* is nothing but discrimination against the female population and an abuse of their human dignity and right. Some may argue that cultural relativism makes *Trokosi* an acceptable social control mechanism for cultures that practice it (Ansong, 2003; Anthony, 2008; Gakleazi, 1998). However, it is common knowledge that abuse and inhumane treatment of any person falls outside the domains of cultural relativism. Such practices constitute violations of basic human right and lower the image and social status of the abused. So, too, are these females.

Educational Imbalance in Ghana

The general cultural perception of Ghanaians, especially in the rural areas, about formal education and the need for academic mobility does not favor the female group. In fact, in some circles, women are excluded in such discussions (Sutherland-Addy, 2002; Tanye, 2008). Since traditional and cultural expectations limit the roles of women to wives and homemakers, the acquisition of basic education will fine-tune their customary socialization, grooming them into good homemakers and bearers of children. Tanye (2008) recently investigated barriers to female education within sub-Saharan Africa and observed that traditional culture shapes a discriminatory orientation in the people and plays a major role in the fewer advocacies for female education in Ghana as in other parts of the sub region.

Ghana, like any other modern civilization, values formal education and sees it as an empowerment for socio-economic emancipation. But as seen earlier in this review, while the Ghanaian culture accepts this as true, traditional cultural conscience encourages this opportunity only for men while women are discouraged from pursuing higher education. Since higher education places them in blue color jobs and not in the full-time-unpaid-homemaker job, the pursuit of higher education is not often recommended for the girl-child (Actual Women Manifesto by Abantu for Development, Ghana, 2004; Agyeman Rawlings, 1998; Tanye, 2008). This fact is reflected in the data available on the ratio of men to women who receive formal education in Ghana from the Ghana Living Standard Survey of 2000 (GLSS, 2000) and also GLSS, 2008 (see Table 4). For instance, it was reported that only about 55.9 % of women as against 78.9 % of men have some kind of formal education. This means that about 44.1% of women have no formal education or never been to school. This figure doubles that of males who have never been to school.

Table 4. *Percentage of 15 Years and Older by Educational Attainment and Sex*

Level of Educational Attainment	%			Estimates (millions)		
	Male	Female	Both	Male	Female	Both
Never been to school	22.3	38.3	30.8	1.4	2.7	4.1
Less than MSLC/BECE	16.2	17.9	17.1	1.0	1.3	2.3
MSLC/BECE/VOC	43.5	34.1	38.6	2.7	2.4	5.1
Secondary or higher	17.9	9.7	13.6	1.1	0.7	1.8
Total	100.0	100.0	100.0	6.3	7.0	13.3

Note. Data obtained from the Ghana Living Standards Statistical Survey (2008); MSLC = Middle School Leaving Certificate; BECE = Basic Education Certificate Examination (elementary level educations); VOC = Vocational Training School (second cycle level education)

The imbalance in this distribution becomes even more concerning in view of the gender ratio in the population distribution of Ghana, where women outnumber men by a 3.09 % margin with 51.5 % women compared to 48.5 % men. One would expect that, with women outnumbering men in the general population distribution, the percentage of women in schools would outnumber that of men. That this is not the case raises a lot of questions (see Table 5). Arguments from other studies expatiated on the lack of encouragement for the girl-child to pursue higher education. These studies argued that it is because higher education reduces their market value of being marriageable (Minkah-Premo, 2001; Sutherland-Addy, 2002; Tanye, 2008). Education, it is believed, has the potential of removing these wife-materials from the home and turning them into paid employees of the formal sector (Actual Women Manifesto by Abantu for Development, Ghana, 2004; Minkah-Premo, 2001; Tanye, 2008). If cultural socialization does turn Ghanaian men into desirers of homemaker-wives over skilled professionals, then the pursuit of higher education will obviously become a cautious endeavor for family-oriented women. Consequently, they may desist from pursuing academic mobility.

Table 5. *Percentage of Adult Literacy Rates by Gender and Locality*

Sex	Urban Accra	Rural Urban	Other All	Rural Coastal	Rural Forest	Rural Savannah	All	Total
Male	88.3	75.1	79.7	65.2	62.1	30.9	51.0	62.7
Female	73.7	53.0	59.6	33.4	33.9	14.2	26.7	40.3
Total	80.8	63.2	69.0	48.2	47.2	22.2	38.2	50.9

Note. Data obtained from the: GLSS 5, Ghana Statistical Service (2008)

The figures in Tables 4 and 5 show evidence buttressing the fact that women do not have a fair strike at educational opportunities as their male counterparts. These statistics show no significant improvement in the number of uneducated women in the country. Thus, the data drawn from the Ghana Living Standard Statistical Survey (2008) revealed that the percentage of women with no education only dropped by 5.8 %. According to data from the GLSS (2008) in Table 4, about half the adult population of Ghana, representing 6.4 million, neither attended school nor ever completed Junior Secondary School (JSS). Out of this non-school population, women formed about twice (2.7 million) the percentage of men (1.4 million) never attending school. Compounding the problem is the fewer numbers of women (0.7 million) than men (1.1 million) with second cycle education or anything higher than that.

Generally, higher percentage of Ghanaians from ages 6 to 25 living in urban areas attend schools compared to those living in rural areas. Table 5 shows that, irrespective of the locality, the literacy rate of Ghanaians is always disproportionately distributed with males outnumbering the females. As evident also in Table 5, the imbalance reported gave about 62.7% males as against 40.3% female as literates of the Ghanaian society. Table 6 however reports current data on school attendance by sex, age, and regional locality. What is evident in these data is the significant difference of school attendance between the sexes for all the ages across the various regions and for the yearly differences (see Tables 6, 7, and 8). For children between ages of 6 and 11, representing primary and lower middle school education, there is about equal percentages of school attendance representing the total average percentages across all regions. The figures for males begin to rise as the educational mobility surges while the figures for females drop with the rise in male figures (see also Table 9).

Table 6. *Percentage of School Attendance by Region, Age, and Gender*

Region	6 – 11		12 – 15		16 – 18		19 – 25		6 – 25		Total
	Male	Female	Male	Female	Male	Female	Male	Female	Male	Female	
Ashanti	97.7	95.6	98.0	94.1	97.4	94.4	94.5	89.6	97.0	93.5	95.2
B-Ahafo	89.8	91.4	95.3	91.8	87.3	92.8	90.5	76.9	90.8	88.0	89.4
Central	7.3	96.5	99.6	97.7	100.0	96.6	95.3	90.4	97.8	93.3	96.9
Eastern	93.3	92.7	98.6	96.8	94.8	95.5	96.7	88.8	95.5	93.1	94.3
Gt-Accra	92.5	93.4	98.1	97.4	97.7	93.7	96.5	91.9	95.8	93.7	94.7
Northern	61.1	57.4	63.7	57.9	52.7	54.8	54.1	31.7	59.2	50.0	54.7
Up/East	66.4	63.9	58.3	67.7	64.9	56.4	64.1	41.5	63.8	58.2	61.2
Up/West	65.5	69.2	68.9	69.3	65.5	66.7	57.2	49.0	64.5	63.8	64.1
Volta	80.0	82.0	97.6	85.5	93.7	89.3	92.1	80.4	88.5	83.6	85.9
Western	94.0	93.7	98.9	94.5	95.5	92.2	92.8	81.1	95.3	90.8	93.0
Total	86.1	86.2	90.4	88.5	87.6	87.3	87.8	77.3	87.8	84.5	86.1

Note. Data obtained from the Ghana Living Standards Statistical Survey (2008)

Table 7. *Gross Enrollment Rate by Sex: 1980/81–1991/92 and 1996/97–1999/00: National Figures in Percent*

Year	Girls	Boys	Totals
1980/81	75.67	87.93	81.82
1981/82	77.03	90.45	83.76
1982/83	77.43	91.35	84.41
1983/84	78.17	92.69	85.45
1984/85	78.52	93.14	85.85
1985/86	78.53	92.29	85.07
1986/87	78.54	92.27	85.42
1987/88	76.98	90.09	83.55
1988/89	76.50	88.76	82.65
1989/90	78.67	87.87	83.28
1990/91	80.75	92.02	86.40
1991/92	75.94	84.43	80.21
1996/97	76.05	83.28	79.67
1997/98	75.57	81.48	78.53
1998/99	79.70	86.20	85.00
1999/00	81.10	86.50	83.80

Note. Data adapted from "Impact Assessment Study of the Girls' Education Programme in Ghana" by E. Sutherland-Addy, 2002; originally sourced from Ministry of Education (MOE), SRIMPR Division.

Table 8. *Percentage of Gross Admission at the Primary and Junior Secondary Schools by Sex: Regional 1996/97 – 1999/00*

| Year | 1996/1997 | | 1997/98 | | 1998/99 | | 1999/00 | |
Regions	Boys	Girls	Boys	Girls	Boys	Girls	Boys	Girls
Ashanti	88.6	83.5	88.7	84.6	92.6	87.8	93.6	87.9
Brong-Ahafo	82.2	79.7	84.0	82.9	77.8	78.4	77.0	78.5
Central	92.0	90.0	86.2	86.8	92.5	91.9	95.1	94.0
Eastern	81.2	80.3	76.8	79.0	78.2	77.6	78.8	78.8
Gt. Accra	73.2	67.1	65.4	61.1	64.2	58.2	72.0	66.1
Northern	79.1	52.5	85.4	58.1	103.7	74.5	98.5	77.2
Upper East	77.1	58.9	69.4	58.0	86.8	74.1	84.8	76.5
Upper West	75.6	60.4	6.9	62.2	86.5	76.8	80.8	74.6
Volta	93.1	90.1	93.6	88.8	98.7	93.6	93.1	87.7
Western	85.2	83.2	82.9	81.1	87.6	86.9	90.9	88.8
National	83.3	76.1	81.5	75.6	86.2	79.7	86.5	81.1

Note. Data adapted from Sutherland-Addy, 2002. [This data was originally obtained from MOE, SRIMPR Division].

Table 9. *Percentage of Gross Enrollment at Primary and JSS Levels by Sex: 1992/93 to 1999/00*

| | Primary | | | JSS | | |
Year	Boys	Girls	Total	Boys	Girls	Total
1992/93	83.71	71.43	77.58	67.44	48.90	58.18
1993/94	84.07	72.19	78.14	68.17	50.23	59.21
1994/95	81.28	70.51	75.90	66.74	50.65	58.71
1995/96	79.70	69.50	74.61	66.49	51.33	58.93
1996/97	81.54	71.54	76.55	65.56	51.60	58.59
1997/98	76.83	68.61	72.53	57.66	51.36	54.51
1998/99	77.10	68.60	72.80	63.80	52.30	58.10
1999/00	79.80	71.60	75.70	64.20	53.30	58.80

Note. Data adapted from Sutherland-Addy, 2002. [Originally obtained from MOE, SRIMPR Division].

Public Sector Administration

As shown earlier in Table 7, enrollment figures do not hold any hope for a better future, as figures show no significant improvement of more girls being educated and prepared for the top level managerial positions in the country. Even though the tables above do not show significant evidence of women closing the gap with men, the proportion of women receiving education does not commensurate with women figures in positions of leadership either. This disparity exists in spite of the Ghanaian constitutional legislation against discrimination of any sort, especially along gender lines. There is no deliberate policy in place to enforce structures of equity between men and women. For a country whose population distribution of men to women is 48.5% and 51.5%, respectively, which gives a sex ratio of 94 males to every 100 females, and with about less than 50% of its females as educated as its males, nothing short of discrimination explains the underrepresentation of women in leadership positions. According to the International Finance Corporation's (IFC) report to the World Bank (Voices of Women Entrepreneurs in Ghana, 2007), only 10% of women are in public offices.

The parliament (the legislative arm of government) is one of the three arms of government in the Ghanaian democracy. Since the 1993 of the fourth republic till 2009 of the fifth republic, of a total of 212 parliamentarians, only an average of about 20.2 being 9.5% of the seats were ever occupied by women.

Table 10 also illustrates the underrepresentation of women in decision-making in one of the most nationally representative bodies of the Ghanaian people. For the governments of 1993, 1997, and 2001, only 19 (9%) out of the 200 parliamentary seats were occupied by women. The 2001 government saw an increase in the number of seats with a corresponding rise in the number of women representation. Twenty-five out of the 230 parliamentary seats fell to women. As though this was something to ignite hopes for greater female representation in the Ghanaian legislative assembly. Unfortunately, the sudden drop from the 25 seats to the traditional 19 female seats during the parliamentary election in the following government of 2009 sends chilling waves of the reminder that the Ghanaian culture has a long way to go in according women the trust of leadership responsibilities.

The Council of State is the advisory body that counsels the president on important decisions pertaining to crucial issues of his governance. Only 16% of the 1997 council of state were women. On a much lower level of the political spectrum, grassroots democracy became the agenda of the 1997 government. To give practical credence to their slogans, the Ghanaian government decentralized political power and governance of the people to the districts in the country. These districts are headed by

Table 10. *Representation of Women in the Ghanaian Parliament from 1993-2009*

Year Year	Number of Available Seats in Parliament	Number of Seats Held by Women	% of Seats Held by Women
1993	200	19	9.50
1997	200	19	9.50
2001	200	19	9.50
2005	230	25	10.90
2009	230	19	8.26
Average	212	20	9.50

Note. Data adopted from, "Women in Politics and Public Life in Ghana". Accra: Friedrich-Ebert Foundation by Friedrich-Ebert & B. Allah-Mensah, 2005. Ghana Statistical Survey Report of the Fifth Round [GLSS 5] (2008)

District Chief Executives (DCE), who are nominated by the President himself. In 2002, of the Fourth Republic, 14,141 candidates registered to contest the District Assembly elections (Center for Democratic Development, 2003). Out of the 14,141 registered candidates, only 981 were females. The total number for all candidates dropped to 13,590 due to withdrawals, disqualifications, and deaths in some cases. For this final total that went into the election, only 7.1% of the 13,590 candidates were women. Prior to this time, the female appointees by the president to the District Chief Executive positions in 1998 were only 12 out of the

110 positions. All these figures indicate that women are less trusted with leadership responsibilities and their ability, competence, and value as equal competitors with their male counterparts are being questioned.

Acher (2002) found this situation frustrating because the very government that calls for affirmative action in balancing the gender disparities (at least) in public sectors does not show any commitment to changing the status quo as reflected in the appointments of District Chief Executives for grass root democracy. Some of the government efforts identified by Acher included attempts made by the Kufour government of 2000. According to Archer, the creation of two new ministries called the Ministry of Women and Children's Affairs and the Ministry of Education's Girl-Child Education Unit and also the establishment of the Women's Endowment Fund, aimed at assisting women entrepreneurs, among other things, were all laudable efforts. However, the apparent failure of government to translate into practicalities the intents of these efforts leaves one to ask the question if government also endorses the culturally supported female subordination?

The Ghanaian Response to Gender Inequity

The concerns expressed by previous studies about the issue of gender discrimination in Ghana centers mainly on why the problem of gender inequities still prevails and why the lack of serious efforts at eradicating it. Of greater concern are the not-so-promising-efforts of governments at curbing out this problem that has created inertia of corrective efforts at the issue of discrimination against women in general (Awumbila, 2001; Chao, 1999; Ofei-Aboagye, 1994; Oheneba-Sakyi, 1999). In sub-Saharan Africa, the common explanation often given to accommodate the under-representation of women in administrative positions is that the discriminatory disposition toward women is a vestige of the traditional sub-Saharan Ghanaian culture, reinforced by colonialism (Awumbila, 2001; Ofei-Aboagye, 1994). Whether this assertion by scholars is true or not evidence from the reviewed literature shows that the efforts of post-colonial Ghana at balancing the gender equation leaves much to be desired.

In recent years, the Ghanaian government has initiated some concrete but loosely monitored legal provisions aimed at propagating equitable treatment of people, irrespective of their gender, race, socio-economic status (SES), and religious affiliations (Amoako-Nuama, 1999; Friedrich-Ebert-Stiftung & Allah-Mensah, 2005; Gender equality and social institutions in Ghana, n.d.; Ofori, 2008). The two most prominent steps taken by the government to address the issue of gender inequities for the citizens of Ghana were The 1992 Republican Constitution and the National Commission for Civil Education (NCCE). While the 1992 Constitution unequivocally declares the equality of all citizens in all spheres of the socio-economic and political life of Ghanaians as mandatory, the NCCE was to ensure awareness and *conscientization* of citizens about all the provisions and responsibilities of the 1992 Republican Constitution. These major provisions notwithstanding, the problem of gender inequity still persists (Friedrich-Ebert-Stiftung & Allah-Mensah, 2005).

Previous research that investigated the scope of discrimination against women have focused mainly on the structural issues of gender inequities such as the imbalance in the occupancy of leadership positions that favors men over women (Actual Women Situation in Ghana, 2004; Bond, 2005; Chao, 1999; Friedrich-Ebert-Stiftung & Allah-Mensah, 2005). These studies attempted explanations of the reason for the gender inequities but failed to examine the internal factors such as ideological beliefs underlying the dynamics of interaction between the few women leaders and the subordinates who work under them. In other words, researchers stopped short of asking the questions about how the few women leadership position are treated by the patriarchal culture? Or which other factors, aside cultural norms and institutional practices, underlie the individual's behavioral disposition in his or her willingness to relate with his or her female boss?

It has been observed that cultures that are patriarchal characteristically do encourage male supremacy over their female counterparts, thus promoting female subordination across the dynamics of the social spectrum (Amos-Wilson, 1999; Awumbila, 2001; Briles, 1999). In the professional arena, such cultures tend to solely endorse men for leadership positions, thereby limiting the status of women to subservient and subordinate positions (Fagenson, 1993). As noted by Awumbila, (2001). Role-play within such structures is often defined along gender stereotypical lines. There are specific roles for women according to cultural expectations as there are for men. And while men tend to be culturally oriented towards leadership roles such as head of the family, decision-maker, and the executor of justice (punishments and rewards), women are trained to assume service-rendering or subservient roles such as domestic servants, providers of family's emotional needs, and often have to defer to their male counterparts in times of decision-making and leadership responsibilities (Awumbila, 2001; Ofei-Aboagye, 1994).

Like Ghana, other patriarchal societies across the world exhibit similar features. Discussing the issue of women's status from the cultural perspective of the American patriarchy, Briles (1999) also emphasized the point on the issue of culturally supported male superiority when stating the following:

> It is not unusual for women to still get the message that they really aren't first class citizens... Pervasive stereotypes about women include that they are not as strong, as capable or as smart as men; that they are emotionally weak, dependent and easily victimized. Along with these generalizations follow the ideas that women need men to take care of them, and they are not whole without men in their lives. As a result, ... women should put others first; and women should be seductive and physically attractive to get a man. (p. 18)

Briles' study named possible behavior patterns likely to emerge from these "overbearing stereotypical expectations." Such behavior patterns may include, (a) women devaluing their own work and that of other women, (b) women failing to take pride in their own accomplishments, often settling for less than what they really worth, (c) women denying that sexism exists, including their own and discounting their own thinking and opinions, (d) women deferring to men during important decision-making, (e) women focusing more on their physical attractiveness as more important than their personal worth and contributions, and (f) women allowing men to touch them or have sex with them even when they do not want to engage in sexual relations. Findings such as these, point to the fact that even some women accept and express a less egalitarian view of gender ideology, thus subscribing to traditional gender ideological beliefs of female subordination and male superiority. Women who express such beliefs may view the occupancy of leadership positions by a woman as a breach of a status quo and could resent it.

Indeed, a study of the literature on the status of women vis-à-vis gender inequities shows significant evidence of discrimination against women in general and, headmistresses, in particular (Amoakohene, 2004; Etter-Lewis, 2000; Oduro & MacBeath, 2003; Stephens, 2000). In Ghana, until recently, only few of the first and second cycle institutions have had headmistresses. Where this is possible, chances are that such schools are female-only parochial institutions built and manned by churches and religious congregations of missionary heritage. Now, more than ever before, more and more schools are being run by headmistresses. No more are these schools only parochial but also public and sometime private (in Ghana private schools simply refer to those set up and run by individuals; public schools are government established schools).

According to Tedrow and Rhoads, (1999), in a society where occupancy of managerial positions is thought to be a male prerogative, female managers have a difficult task establishing themselves as heads and even harder task adjusting to this reality psychologically. This and other studies have identified Ghana, a Sub-Saharan African country, as one of such societies that support male hegemony over female subordination (see also Awumbila, 2001; Friedrich-Ebert-Stiftung & Allah-Mensah, 2005). This culturally significant foible cuts across sectors of the job market including even the education sector. Professional interaction between the leader and the led in such a context may be characterized by uncertainties, suspicions, and frequent conflicts.

As noted by some researchers (Awumbila, 2001; Friedrich-Ebert-Stiftung & Allah-Mensah, 2005), men dominate hierarchical positions in Ghana's sociopolitical environment. Even in selecting leaders for political positions, among others, women are not given equal consideration with male candidates (Awumbila, 2001). Thus, there is general consensus among scholars that the population dominating the fields of decision-making processes in Ghana are males (Amos-Wilson, 1999; Friedrich-Ebert-Stiftung & Allah-Mensah, 2005; King, 2006) (see also Table 5). In the given situation, the earned authority of female heads could often be a threat to men's socio-culturally held normative notion of the favored male hegemony. Consequently, traditionalists (especially men) who cannot stand this power twist, often show their resentments in words or actions to intimidate these female heads (Oduro & MacBeath, 2003).

Unrelated to the Ghanaian situation and yet cognate to its concerns, the Interstate School Leaders Licensure Consortium (ISLLC) of United States has proposed seven standards for the effective management of schools in a bid to achieving the success of teaching and learning. The sixth of these ISLLC standards discusses, among other things, the importance of school climate in ensuring effective performances by teachers and students. According to the ISLLC standards, respect for one another and treating all individuals with fairness, dignity and ethical considerations, based on merits, are not just valued options but also necessary ingredients for civil interaction between teachers and their principals (headmistresses/headmasters).

Also emphasized by the ISLLC standards for the successful management of schools are, the "culture of shared values, beliefs, and traditions, in which the responsibilities and contributions of each individual are acknowledged" (Hessel & Holloway, 2002, p. 47). The general message of the ISLLC standards therefore is that respect for individual's abilities should be based on merit (and not on some personal ideological beliefs of prejudice). This understanding should guide professional interaction in the day-to-day management of schools.

Writing about women in management positions, Fagenson (1993) once posed the following questions: "How can they manage having a family and a satisfying career?" "How can they ensure that their experiences and concerns will be taken seriously, and given priority, and that each, individually, will be treated with respect by the male community?" (p. 3). Even though these hypothetical questions were asked to reexamine evidence of gender discrimination within the western American culture, their relevancy for many a patriarchal society, such as the Ghanaian society of sub-Saharan Africa, cannot be overemphasized. Indeed, in any society where women's ascendancy to managerial positions is seen as a breach of the cultural status quo, Fagenson's questions may be reechoed. Such may be the case for the few female heads of schools in Ghana as investigated by Oduro and MacBeath (2003). A legitimate concern, congruent to Fagenson's questions, is how willing and tolerant is the Ghanaian patriarchal society in accepting the wave of women becoming school administrators and managers; and how willing is that society in contracting for social collaboration with these female bosses so as to ensure an effective, collegial and professional school environment?

The Struggle of the Ghanaian Headmistresses

As mentioned earlier, it is a challenge to statistically evaluate the gender balance of school administrators in Ghana for any empirical investigation. When a search was conducted electronically for studies on problems of gender inequities in school management in Ghana, the result was startling. Only one article published in 2003 specifically devoted about a page in their qualitative research discussing specific discrimination against female headteachers in rural and urban schools (Oduro & MacBeath, 2003). The literature may have little to say about the struggles of the female heads of schools in the mist of active patriarchy in Ghana. However, indices from the culture about discrimination and misrepresentation of women (whether at the workplace or outside it) are inklings of such struggles on the part of women in establishing their authority over their subordinates.

As a result of these findings, Oduro and MacBeath (2003) conducted a study on socially endemic evidence of discriminations against women in school administration. The study, among other things, revealed confirmatory confessions concerning the struggles of these women school heads in establishing their authority as administrators of their institutions in the midst of active and enduring patriarchy. The study also revealed that teachers, especially the elderly ones, view their female heads as at their footstool regardless of their position as heads. The main purpose of the Oduro and MacBeath's study was to examine the tensions Ghanaian headteachers face in trying to resolve traditional and tribal expectations with 'Western' conceptions of leadership roles and competencies. A reflection on teachers' perceptions of female headteachers vis-à-vis gender stereotyping exposed teachers' general aversion towards the idea of women being heads of their institution. As reported by Oduro and MacBeath:

> Two women heads in this study complained that their initial days in their schools were difficult because they happened to be the first female headteachers in those schools. As a result, the male teachers, especially the older ones, found it difficult to cooperate with them. One of the two women heads said that the School Management Chair (SMC) did not take it lightly when she expressed opinions contrary to his. The chairman assumed that she, as the only woman present, would accept whatever the male members agreed on. As a result, she said she was once shouted at by the chairman with a local expression that literally translates as "Don't forget you're a woman; soften yourself" (pp. 445- 446).

The last words of the above quote '...soften yourself', simply means *'subordinate yourself to us* (men)'. The confessions above epitomized the general attitude towards women in the Ghanaian culture and could be generalized for the rest of sub-Saran Africa; women, no matter their social status, must subordinate themselves to men. Further revelations from the Oduro and MacBeath's study indicated that while female headteachers' oppositions in the rural schools came from male subordinates, the female headteachers living in the urban schools contended not only with male oppositions but also with the opposition of their female subordinates. A number of reasons were advanced for this sex twist. It was observed that because women were considered weak, emotionally fragile, physically vulnerable, and ill-equipped with survival skills posting them to the rural areas (where life is difficult and challenging), is often discouraged. As a result their study made use of more female teacher samples from the urban schools while very few female teachers (save for the female headteachers of the study) participated in the study from the rural samples. Another reason gauged out of this study was that both men and women teachers preferred male headteachers to female heads because they underestimate the ability of these women heads to effectively manage their schools (even though, evidence of cooperation from some male teachers was experienced by some of the female heads of the study).

Another female headteacher of the Oduro and MacBeath's (2003) study reported that her attempt to enforce professional discipline for teachers in her school (no lateness, coming drunk to school, late submission of lesson notes), was met with strong opposition, especially from the female teachers, who considered her approach as being rude. Whether such opposition from fellow women (teachers) is a function of they being less egalitarian is yet to be investigated. Such conflicts within school environment could become recipes for tensions that could lead to the creation of social distance between teachers and their headmistresses. In the economy of school management the cooperation of teachers with their heads is pivotal. Teachers form the building blocks of school management ideas and strategies; a powerhouse into which headteachers tap to create an enabling school milieu. Any attempt to dissociate this powerhouse from the reach of the administrative head will result in undermining all efforts at school effectiveness.

In the year 2002, the news media was full of headlines such as "Hundreds of Women Take to Streets," "Tradition Trumps Progressive Laws," "Dearth of Women in Government and Obstacle to Enforcement," (www.afrol.com/Categories/Women/ profiles/ghana_women.htm).

A paragraph in one of the news items under the caption, *Hundreds of Women Take to Streets,* touched the crux of the matter when it reported that the commanding officer for the Women and Juvenile Unit of the police force, as saying:

> The abuse of women in Ghana is alarming… There is too much superiority complex among their male counterparts. They think women cannot think on their own; they think women are part of their property. Some Ghanaian men even think women don't have sense and so

they should decide what a woman should do. (www.afrol.
com/Categories/ Women/profiles/ghana_women.htm)

This news item concluded that a climate of acceptance of violence
against women in Ghana appears to have been created by the permissive
culture and is still prevailing. If indeed the assertion of these news items,
that Ghanaian women are perceived by society as a group who cannot
think on their own, who do not have the sense to decide, and hence should
have men decide for them is true, then it stands to reason that it will be
difficult for such a society to see women in leadership roles with men
as their subordinates. In the circumstances then, social distance – here
defined as the interpersonal relationship born out of the willingness or
non-willingness to contract social ties with female bosses – may ultimately
arise as a corollary.

For a better comprehension of the issue of discriminatory attitude
toward female school heads and its ramifications for collaboration between
teachers and their female heads in Ghana, it is important to expand our
discussion cross-culturally. A look at the issue from other such patriarchal
cultures will help our understanding of the sub-Saharan Ghanaian
situation, which is not to be isolated, anyway. Consequently, we will
consider some of the findings from cultures of America, Asia, Middle East,
and South Africa. These studies investigated the struggles and successes of
women school heads in the midst of active patriarchy.

Cross-cultural Evidence of the Struggle of Female School Administrators

Some of the studies that examined the perception people have of
female school heads in America were the works of Bloom and Erlandson
(2003), Fennell (1999), Foster, Arnt, and Honkola (2004), and Loder
(2005). Bloom and Erlandson (2003) examined the struggle for equitability
and recognition by some African American women school principals
within the traditional administrative structures of the American culture.
Participants included three urban city school principals who shared their

experiences of leadership practices and the community response to their leadership. Research questions for Bloom and Erlandson's study included items such as: How do the experiences of three African American women principals reflect the impact of gender and race on leadership practice in urban schools? The domains examined in this study were the influence of collective consciousness and cultural consciousness on how these women contended with the male dominant culture.

Even though religious experience and family support were said to have aided these women principals in contending well with the male dominant culture, the presence of discrimination was not ruled out (at least by the researchers) in the experiences of theses participants. In another study, Troder (2005) also examined the struggle of some African American women school principals from a life course perspective. The focus of this study was on the multiple influences of race, gender, and generation on leadership orientation. This exploratory study revealed that the authority of these women principals was challenged not only by their subordinates but also by parents of their students when they brought about changes within their buildings. Even though it was not explicitly stated that such hostilities were due to elements of gender discrimination, it was, however, noted that prior attitudes of the parents towards the male principals, who were the predecessors of these women principals, were different (respectful). These male principals were well accepted by the people (Troder, 2005). A probable explanation to this difference (though not inferred here) is gender stereotypical discrimination. An interesting revelation also observed from the American front is the fact that some women also turn to participate sometimes in their own oppression than men do of them (Foster, Arnt & Honkola, 2004). In other words, some women from the American culture still hold on to ideological beliefs that perceive women as subordinates to men and vulnerable to gender stereotypical discrimination.

A look at the Asian culture also has interesting revelations of research importance. Thus, Shum and Cheng (1997) investigated different styles of administrative approach by some female principals, vis-à-vis sex role orientation, and the kind of response evoked from their teachers as favorable and not favorable. Their findings demonstrated that teachers favorably perceived female principals with androgynous style of leadership whereas those with masculine authoritative orientation met with unfavorable perceptions. Inklings from such observations point to the fact that when women assume roles leadership they must retain their feminine touch and approach to be accepted by subordinates. Those with masculine demeanor and approach in their leadership styles are resented. It appears that when women assume leadership roles a sacred zone appears to be violated and people's reaction to such violation is disapproval and disenfranchisement of the female actors (women administrators). Taking a global look at the Asian situation, Tang (2004) went as far as to conclude that only an injunction with United Nations' authority behind it, in terms of law, is needed to eradicate the systemic discrimination of the women population.

The Arabic culture is not an exception. Shapira, Arar, and Azaiza (2010) more recently observed that the culture of male hegemony and female subordination is so strong within Middle Eastern Arabic cultures that it is common for women to sacrifice their promotion for male subordinates to assume them in order not to offend sensitivity about the traditional status quo of male dominance. Thus, Shapira, Arar, and Azaiza (2010) observed that even though women outnumber men in the teaching field, when it comes to promotion into administrative positions, Arab women teachers are "expected to forfeit their professional promotion for the benefit of men's advancement, to avoid undermining the patriarchal structure of Arab society and the threats to men's status" (p. 705). They however concluded that the women in their study evaded the consequences of such breaches of the traditional status quo and escaped the gender-based discrimination against them because they adopted feminine managerial styles of caring, concern, and empowering-others-strategy instead of the masculine orientation type. This finding is consistent with similar findings from the Asian and American cultures as observed also by Fennell (1999) and Shum and Chang (1997).

Cognate to the Ghanaian context is the study from South Africa. Like the Ghanaian culture, the South African patriarchal culture is also dominated with male school administrators. The few women rising through the ranks and files of the school system into administrative positions have barriers to reckon with (Thakathi & Lemmer, 2002). Thakathi and Lemmer investigated female school heads' communication styles and how that impact teachers' perception of these women heads. In a sense, this study examined the struggle of female principals in establishing their authority as heads within a male dominant culture. Their findings revealed that tact and cautious strategies needed to be employed by these minority women principals in order to be accepted as heads within their schools. These strategies were seen as necessary tools to equipoise the attitude of subordinates, who often discriminate against women administrators who come across as projecting themselves as bosses in their communication styles. These assertions by Thakathi and Lemmer are, however, at variance with what later research finds.

Some recent studies from America (Christman & McClellan, 2008), Bangladesh in Asia (Zafarullah, 2000) and South Africa (Moorosi, 2010) on the struggles of women in school administration at first and second cycle institutions, for instance, are symmetrical in their findings and yet with different conclusion. These researchers concluded that women who became leaders in educational administration did so as survivors of the narrow margins of their administrative ranks, and only by adopting certain masculine characteristics such as resilience and the determination to succeed and never to accept failures. Such conclusions lend credence to the argument that for women to attain and survive such leadership positions they occupy, they must adopt masculine styles of leadership strategies to stand the vagaries of their professional environment which views such positions as male-typed.

The common denominator for the two conclusions is that theoretically, society still gender-stereotypes to the disadvantage of women, even if they earned their leadership positions by the merit of their qualifications. All of the cross-cultural studies reviewed in this research indicate that the struggle of women school heads can be daunting even though some of their efforts are not without success. There are times when female principals have to adopt androgynous managerial styles that shied away from masculine authoritative styles; employing caring and inclusive strategies of leadership models, so as to be met with less antagonism. There are other times when masculine administrative styles have to be adopted to prove the resilience of the female administrator so as to stand the vagaries of male dominance to succeed as female bosses.

What is evident here is that in all of these cultures, sex-role orientation (gender ideological belief) plays a role in how women school administrators are perceived by their teachers in their roles as heads. The barriers experienced by women in school management careers across world cultures are startling. The paradox lies in the fact that this phenomenal social disenfranchisement of women persists as programs of gender equity become the vogue of world governments. Some scholars share the consensus that the barriers created for these women heads of schools are natural derivatives of the tradition-long-cultures that espouse the under representation of women in leadership roles (Amos-Wilson, 1999; Koslowsky & Schwarzwald, 2006). Another observation of scholars is that society is unfamiliar with women assuming leadership roles; this estrangement of women in leadership position, hence, is the natural result of society's reaction to the lack of familiarity with the new (strange) wave of women taking positions otherwise belonging to men (Andes, 1992; Gazso, 2003; Giannopoulos, Conway & Mendelson, 2005; Rashotte & Webster, 2005). Other scholars also concluded from their investigations that the consideration of social contexts is important in determining attitudes towards women in leadership (Collard, 2001; Gazso, 2003; Keshet, Kark, Pomerantz-Zorin, Koslowsky, & Schwarzwald, 2006).

Whether the determination of gender-based discrimination stems from a reaction to the non-familiarity with a particular sex assuming a non-traditional role, or as a result of a social contextual orientation, Gazso (2004) insisted that the basic underlying factor to all gender-based discrimination is the gender ideological beliefs of actors. The conclusion I can draw from all of these studies is that the struggle of women heads of school administration is homogeneous in patriarchal societies regardless of cultural or geographical location.

Whereas some studies attempt the argument that culturally supported gender ideological beliefs are no more viable determinants of discrimination against women in management positions (Collard, 2001), a recent study by Shapira, Arar, and Azaiza (2011) seems to be refuting the above argument and sends the world an unpleasant reminder that gender ideological beliefs are still the strong undercurrents of negative attitudes toward women in school administration. Shapira et al. (2011) analyzed data from Israeli Arab communities about the community acceptance of female school principals in the midst of enduring patriarchy. Participants of their study included teachers (both male and female), local community leaders, and people drawn from the community itself. Also included in the sample were the extended and immediate family members of the seven female principals involved for the study. These women were exceptional in their qualification for the principalship position but had to be tendered for the position. One of the principals described the tender process as a battle incurring wounds that needed to be healed. Another woman felt betrayed by her own "acquaintances on the tender committee." Another woman principal said she was opposed twice by the head of the local council when she won the tender on each of those occasions. The fourth woman principal was also opposed by the head of the local council, who, it is said, attempted to defame her; the fifth woman was scared and almost never applied for the tender but for the encouragement of the Jewish head of the local council; the sixth woman principal stated she functioned under pressure from a male rival.

The oppositions faced by these women were not about their qualifications for the principalship position but, as rightly concluded by Shapira et al. (2011), their entry into this leadership position was seen as a threat to the masculine culture. They were occupying positions of central authority in the community reserved only for men. What is even more interesting about their findings was that, even the family members of these female principals saw their entry into these principal positions as a breach of the cultural norm and therefore resented it. Clearly, there was no consideration for the experience and expertise of these women. It would probably not matter even if they were better qualified than their male competitors. Such publicly expressed aversion across the spectrum of the community within which they worked could create a hostile and challenging work environment for these female principals. This tension has the potential of creating social distance between these communities and their female principals.

To appreciate the function of social distance as a correlate of gender discrimination and how this construct (social distance) fits into teachers' discriminatory attitude towards headmistresses, a discussion of the social distance concept is salient and will be discussed in the next section.

The Conceptualization of Social Distance

Social distance is defined by Parrillo and Donoghue (2005) as the level of acceptance a person feels towards another individual or a member of that person's out-group. Bogardus (1959), one of the originators of the construct, defined social distance as: "the degree of sympathetic understanding that functions between person and person, between person and group, and between group and group" (p. 7). In this study, social distance was conceptualized as the psycho-emotional expression of one's innate perception of the other, and one's willingness to or not to trade social interaction with the other based on those innate perceptions. Social distance then may be understood as an outward expression of one's covert intention of behavioral deposition.

Attitude is a learned or acquired disposition that represents the gamut of a person's experiences and manifests itself in given circumstances, thus predisposing a person to a particular type of behavior (Bergmann, 1988). Discriminatory disposition then potentially leads one to act negatively toward the object of one's discrimination. Triandis (1971), one of the chief proponents of the concept of social distance, further expatiated on disposition and its potentials for behavioral attitude. Triandis stated that human beings act and react to objects and situations based on their perceived notion of what the objects of their action and reaction represent to them and how they understood what was being communicated by these perceived objects.

According to Parrillo and Donoghue (2005), the attitudes people form about others are often nurtured by the cultural experiences within which these individuals live and grow; cultures which shape the idiosyncratic behaviors of these individual actors and give their behaviors meaningful grounds for expression. Social distance, which is the result of an individual's behavioral disposition of the willingness to associate or not to associate with an out-group, may find expression in Perrillo and Donoghue's assumption. A similar argument was made by Triandis and Triandis (1962) in one of their early works on a cross-cultural study of social distance. These scholars concluded that the social distance experienced by an individual towards out-groups is much more a function of the norms of his social group, concerning appropriate behavior towards out-groups, than a function of his particular personality, though certain kinds of personality characteristics function to accentuate conformity to norms. (pp. 19-20)

Drawing from the above conceptual definitions this researcher suggests that in much the same way, the Ghanaian patriarchal culture may be the nurturing ground for teachers' egalitarian beliefs that may determine their degree of interpersonal closeness with their headmistresses.

From the literature reviewed on the cultural situation in Ghana vis-à-vis women's status, it is clear that the Ghanaian culture supports a gender ideology that adheres to the belief in male hegemony over female subordination and, thus, discriminates against women. How significant this is in understanding the professional interaction between teachers and their headmistresses, is of interest to this researcher. As Triandis and Triandis (1988) rightly observed, some social distance phenomena have at their bases elements of hate and/or dislike such as racial discrimination or religious extremism. It is, however, important to note that even though gender discrimination is not necessarily hatred or dislike for the inferior gender, it is disenfranchising of the inferior gender's (the women population) rights and capabilities.

Indeed, gender discrimination or sexism may result from the adherence to a culturally inherited behavioral legacy embedded in the traditional processes of socialization cognate to a person's cultural milieu that stereotypes. Gender discrimination, according to Anderson, (1988), is an institutionalized and internalized vestige of a chauvinistic culture and finds expression in people's every day social interactions. Thus, in any male chauvinistic society, almost everybody grows up believing that men are superior to women; that decision-making is the prerogative of men (Ofei-Aboagye, 1994); and that leadership prerogatives are men's by some natural designs (Sugarman & Frankel, 1996). Those who have these kinds of beliefs are less egalitarian or may be described as traditionalists. The less egalitarian a person is, the more likely that person is in adhering to the patriarchal ideology. Loyalty to a gender ideological belief that looks down on the female group does constitute an indirect latent or albeit deliberate act of discrimination towards the female out-group.

Underlying a person willingness to associate or not to associate with the other of his or her out-group is a kind of pull-and-push force of attraction that pulls a person towards the other or repels a person from his/her out-group (Bogardus, 1959) based on one's desires. To have a better understanding of how social distance can result due to gender discrimination, a discussion of the psychology behind the willingness to and non-willingness to associate (a kind of pull and push effect) is warranted. This pull and push force, known as valence, will be discussed in the paragraphs below.

Valence as a Force of Social Distance

If perceptions bring about acceptance and likeness, then a person becomes attracted to another individual based on some appealing ontological facts, which the observer associates with that other individual. It is this associated facts that may evoke a feeling of attraction as an automatic response on the part of the perceiver (Krieglmeyer, De Houwer, & Deutsch, 2011). According to Krieglmeyer et al., a motivational force, generated by this attraction and likeness, compels the person to react. This motivating force then becomes operational only when the reality, which exists before it, is meaningful enough to evoke a feeling response. For example, a man who likes only blue-eye women may be attracted by a blue-eyed lady and may be motivated to initiate some interaction with her. His attraction is evoked by the presence of blue eyes. In his case then, there has to exist blue eyes for him to be attracted. The presence of blue eyes then becomes meaningful to him and communicates a message (valence) that attracts an automatic response from him.

The above example describes positive valence. Valence may also be negative. Just as positive valence attracts, negative valence may cause a person to withdraw from his/her subject if the conceived notions about that subject (the out-group) breed dislike and repulsion (Triandis, 1971). Thus, valence may be either positive or negative. A person who welcomes another into his/her space illustrates the operation of positive social valence. A person who dissociates him or herself from another in an act of discrimination acts upon negative social valence.

Social valence is goaded by personal and social/cultural forces and manifests itself as sympathy, understanding, acceptance, and at the other extreme of the polarity of human relations, it manifests as jealousy, scorn, misunderstanding, misjudging, hatred, dislike, and rejection (Triandis, 1971). These are demonstrated in a person's attitude toward another of his or her out-group. Since a person's background helps in shaping his or her idiosyncratic life, knowing about a person's worldview helps to attempt a prediction of the likely behaviors of that individual.

Social distance, which is the latitude of social interaction an individual is willing to have with another person, does not happen in a vacuum. It comes about as a result of and is determined by individual's perception of their stimulus person that makes them want to or not want to interact with that stimulus person. To understand the social distance between people, therefore, one needs to understand, first and foremost, the kind of valence that is operating: is it a positive social valence or a negative social valence? A more egalitarian person will have positive valence toward a female boss thereby developing close social distance with her.

A less egalitarian person will have negative valence because there is no effective stimulus to facilitate close interpersonal relationship with his or her female boss (Krieglmeyer et al., 2011). It is the informed proposition of this researcher that people's behavioral dispositions that emanates from their perceived beliefs about their out-group that lead to the formation of a certain behavioral attitude. This attitude ultimately manifests in the creation of social distance between these individuals and their out-group. Another way to explain the phenomenon of social distance is to diagram the potential theoretical relationships between perception, behavioral disposition, attitude, and social distance as illustrated in Figure 1. This assumption for the theoretical relationship linking these dispositions is yet to be established and tested in this exploratory research.

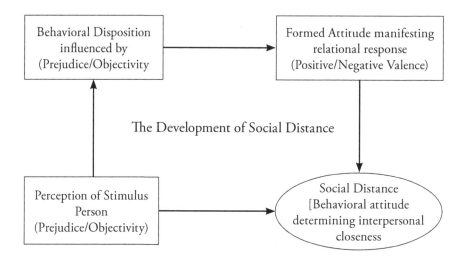

Figure 1. *Theoretical representation of the development of social distance construct*

Note. This theoretical relationship illustrates how individual's perception of his or her stimulus persons (an out-group) leads to the creation of social distance between that individual and the stimulus person.

Some scholars emphasize the fact that people's attitude, because of positive or negative perceptions about their out-groups, is the strongest determinant of social distance (Bernstein, Sacco, Young, Hugenberg, & Cook, 2010; Diekman & Hirnisey, 2007; Herek & Capitanio, 1996; Ko, Judd, & Blair, 2006; Ko, Judd, & Stapel, 2009; Riek, Mania, & Gaertner, 2006). For instance, Bernstein, et al. (2010) found that attitude of rejection (which denotes social distance by negative valence) is the effect of the perceived differences in behavior and characteristics between out-groups and in-groups generating a force of attraction or repulsion. The present study identifies that force to be the degree of egalitarian feeling of the individual teachers in this study.

Triandis (1971), however, found that attitudes are composed of three main components: cognitive (beliefs), affective (feelings), and behavior (actual actions). Cognition may be defined as the awareness of one's state of mind about phenomena or the knowledge of the realities common to a person's milieu within which and by which human behavior may be explained. The affective component of attitudes has to do with feelings that are begotten from the cognitive functions that initiate a connection between a person and the other. The behavior component is then the programmed or natural response of a person based on the person's knowledge of the phenomenon of interest and the perceptions of that person about the phenomenon (Triandis, 1971).

Explaining attitude in terms of these three components, however, makes the measure of attitude very unpredictable. This is because feelings, for example, do not automatically evoke a response of the actor nor does cognition always explain human response or behavior. Hence, an angry person may laugh hysterically to hide his or her anger. Similarly, a belief that something does exist may not necessarily arouse any affection or cause any relational response between the believer and the object of belief. However, a belief in a Deity does evoke a series of attitudes on the part of the believer towards the Deity. In this latter case, belief is seen as shaping one's attitudes. It is the interaction between the beliefs and attitudes, as well as any underlying values or opinions that one may hold that make attitude a difficult thing to measure.

Other scholars also observed that there is a distinction between attitudes and overt behavior (Mueller, 1986; Lemon, 1973; Triandis, 1971; Williamson, 1976). Just because a person expresses feelings about what he or she would do or would not, do does not necessarily mean that he/she will ultimately act out his or her feelings in real life situation. All the above observations are reminders of the fact that the measure of people feelings in determining their behavioral response is often a subjective determination.

The social distance depicted by this study, therefore, is that which expresses one's culturally supported attitudes that subordinate the female group and ascribed to women a subservient status; a status ascription that depicts the female superior as a non-equal to her male counterparts, a less-capable, an unqualified occupier, an oddity, an oddball, and an unorthodox impostor. In a male chauvinistic society of the Ghanaian kind, therefore, statements such as, I will (not) accept as an intimate friend; I will (not) feel comfortable obeying her orders; and I will (not) vote her into a political office, *inter alia*, become significantly relevant in determining the acquiescence of respondents. Such statements reveal whether or not teachers' stated fondness or aversion towards a female school heads depicts, respectively, the willingness to associate or not to associate with her.

In view of the revelations made by the review of the literature, vis a vis the purpose of the study, I will examine in this study the social distance of Ghanaian teachers with their female headmistresses, testing the effects of multiple independent variables (egalitarianism, age, lineage affiliation, and gender of teachers) on the criterion variable (social distance).

Background to the Research Hypotheses

Egalitarianism is defined as teachers' unbiased views and attitude towards their headmistress independent of her sex. In other words, egalitarianism is measured by teachers' stated views on gender roles ascription as to which social functions men and women are expected to perform in the Ghanaian society. Specifically, egalitarianism (egalitarian view of gender ideological belief) expresses equality of persons, irrespective of their sex (Tang, 2004; Koivunen, Rothaupt, & Wolfgram, 2009; Kroska & Elman, 2009; Ui & Matsui, 2007). An adherent of less egalitarian beliefs then holds views about male hegemony with a philosophy of female subordination. Such a person will express views that do not support the idea that the headmistress of his or her school possesses competencies that equal those of a male counterpart. Such stated views, in effect, ascribe leadership roles to men and subservient roles to women (Awumbila, 2001; Ofei-Aboagye, 1994). Based on the above research assertions, it was hypothesized that teachers reporting less egalitarian views of gender ideology would report greater social distance with their headmistresses, while teachers with more egalitarian views would report closer or more intimate social distance with their headmistresses.

Lineage affiliation is defined as teachers' belongingness to either the patrilineal or the matrilineal descents of Ghana. The literature on lineage affiliations in Ghana indicated that women from the matrilineal lineage system, who have inheritance prerogatives traced through them, do enjoy some degree of importance among kinsmen, thus raising their social status above women from the patrilineal systems (Takyi & Broughton, 2006;

Takyi & Gyimah, 2007). Such a woman, cognizant of her importance among her kin, should appreciate her worth to society with some air of equality with others of her society. Consequently, and because of the prominence these women enjoy in the matrilineal society, it will be hypothesized that teachers from the matrilineal descent will report less social distance with their headmistresses in the Ghanaian second cycle institution compared to teachers from the patrilineal descent.

Sex, reported as male or female depending on the respondent's biological sexual identity, is seen in the literature as an important correlate of social distance and/or disenfranchisement of the female stimulus person (Brunner, 2000; Nukunya, 1987; Oduro & MacBeath, 2003; Takyi & Broughton, 2006). It is the observation of all these scholars that men, rather than women, traditionally occupy leadership positions in the Ghanaian socio-politico-administrative circles. The conclusion of all of these scholars suggests that women who occupy this male-typed leadership positions are likely to be resented, especially by their male counterparts.

That male teachers will have greater social distance towards their headmistresses in the Ghanaian second cycle institutions compared to their female teacher counterparts specifically finds notable emphasis in the Oduro and MacBeath's (2003) study. The demonstrated evidence from the Oduro and MacBeath's (2003) study where it was observed that some Ghanaian male teachers (and not female teachers) openly resented the authority of their headmistress, reminding her not to forget the fact that she is still a woman, amply attest to the fact of sexism within the culture. Consequently, it will be hypothesized that the gender of teachers will influence teachers' degree of social distance with their headmistresses.

Age is defined as the reported actual ages of respondents stated in figures. The stated age depicts respondent's age at the time of participating in the survey. The literature review noted, among other studies, the study of Oduro and MacBeath (2003), which observed older (male) teachers resenting the authority of their female heads (headmistresses). It may also be based on the assumption that because of the influence of modernity, the younger generation of teachers are becoming more egalitarian in their views when it comes to gender role expectations while the older generation still hold on to traditional gender role expectations (Amancio, 2002;

Devika, 2006; MacInnes, 1998). Consequently, it will be hypothesized that age will play significant role in influencing teachers' social distance with their headmistresses. That the older the teacher, the less egalitarian he/she will be and the greater the social distance between such a teacher and the headmistress.

In summary, the literature reviewed linked age group differences and gender of respondents to respondents' sex role attitudes (Ui & Matsui, 2007). Anderson and Johnson's (2003) study also found that the younger generation and women are more egalitarian than older generation and men respectively. Evidence linking differentials in lineage ties with women's autonomy among Ghanaians is confirmed by Takyi and Broughton's (2006) study. The strong predictive value of gender ideological belief, among other variables, in investigating views on attitudes toward sex role differentials of workers were the findings of Kroska and Elman (2009). Based on these substantive findings, it will be hypothesized that the four domains of the predictor variables (degree of egalitarianism, lineage affiliation, sex, and age) will directly predict teachers' social distance with their headmistresses in the second cycle institutions of Ghana.

Research Questions and Hypotheses

Two main research questions were addressed in this study. Research question 1 contains five hypotheses and Research question 2 contains one hypothesis.

Research Question 1

Do the degree of egalitarianism, lineage tie, gender, and age of teachers in second cycle institutions in Ghana statistically and practically significantly relate to and predict their perceived social distance towards their headmistress?

Hypothesis 1. It is hypothesized that the degree of egalitarianism, lineage tie, gender, and age of teachers, in second cycle institutions in

Ghana significantly relate to and predict teachers' social distance towards their headmistress.

Hypothesis 2. It is hypothesized that the higher degree of egalitarianism reported by the teachers, the lesser their perceived social distance towards their headmistress.

Hypothesis 3. It is hypothesized that the teachers of matrilineal descent will have lesser-perceived social distance towards their headmistress than their patrilineal counterparts.

Hypothesis 4. It is hypothesized that the female teachers will have lesser-perceived social distance towards their headmistress than the male teachers.

Hypothesis 5. It is hypothesized that the younger the teacher, the lesser the perceived social distance towards their headmistress.

Research Question 2

Are there any differentials in the degree of egalitarianism, lineage tie, gender, and age of teachers in second cycle institutions of Ghana in predicting their social distance with a headmistress? If so, which variable is the strongest predictor of teachers' social distance with their headmistress in second cycle institutions in Ghana: degree of egalitarianism, lineage affiliation, gender, or age?

Hypothesis 6. It is hypothesized that degree of egalitarianism of teachers in second cycle institutions in Ghana will be the strongest predictor of perceived social distance toward a headmistress

CHAPTER III

METHOD

Research Design

A non-experimental multivariate exploratory correlational research design was used in this study. In a correlational design, the intent of the researcher is to examine the relationships between or among variables (Newman, Newman, Brown, & McNeely, 2006). This design is multivariate because the relationship among multiple independent variables and a continuous dependent variable are examined. In multivariate designs, the independent variables can be a combination of variables measured on a categorical or continuous scale (Meyers, Gamst & Guarino, 2006). The independent variables of this study are a combination of both. *Lineage affiliation* and *gender* are categorical, dichotomous variables and the degree of *egalitarianism* and *age* are continuous variables. The dependent or criterion variable, which is teachers' perceived social distance with headmistresses, is a continuous variable.

This study employs a non-experimental design in that the independent variables were not manipulated. This research can also be considered ex post facto. Ex post facto research refers to when the independent variable(s) is naturally occurring or has already occurred and thus cannot be manipulated by the researcher (Gall, Gall, & Borg, 2010; Newman et al., 2006; Newman, Benz, Weis, & McNeil, 1997). Ex post facto research also compares multiple groups but those groups must have already been formed and cannot be manipulated by the researcher (Newman &

McNeil, 1998). The independent variables in this study, which include degree of egalitarianism, lineage system, age, and gender variables, consist of naturally occurring groups and thus were not manipulated by the researcher.

Sampling Method

A multi-level, non-random sampling method was used in this study. Purposive sampling was also used in that the participants had to be teachers in a second-cycle school and/or Teacher Training Colleges (TTC), they have to be born and raised Ghanaians, have a female headmistress as head of their school, and belong to either the patrilineal or matrilineal system of lineage.

In Ghana, it is possible for a person to belong to both lineage systems if a person's father came from the patrilineal society and the mother came from the matrilineal group. Such a person has the privilege of tracing descent along both paternal and maternal lines. Teachers who have dual lineage ties - belonging to both the patrilineal and matrilineal systems - were not included in the final sample. This exclusion is to eliminate the possibility of descent ambivalence in the identification of one's lineage tie.

In all, there are approximately 548 institutions, from which 12 schools were selected. The sample for this study then was drawn from the 12 selected schools. (National Council for Tertiary Education, Statistical Digest for Colleges of Education, 2009/2010; Ghana Education Service: List of Public Senior High Schools, 2010/11). Data on the proportion of gender differentials in headship of schools in Ghana were not readily available. Personal visits to the nation's education headquarters yielded no data identifying which schools were female-headed.

As a result of the lack of data on all second-cycle institutions that were female-headed, judgment sampling was used, in part, to identify which schools were likely to be female-headed. From the NCTESDC data, about 45 teachers, on average, teach in each TTC. This average was computed for all the target schools. For lack of data on the proportion of schools headed by headmistresses, the researcher estimated that 20% of the schools in Ghana were female-headed second cycle institutions. This estimate yielded a total of 110 institutions. This estimate was again based on the national average of 20% female leaders in decision-making positions in the government (GSS, 2008). Multiplying this total estimate by the average number of teachers per each TTCs (45 teachers per school) yielded an approximate total number of 4,950 teachers in these female-headed institutions. This total was the target population for this study from which the sample for this study was drawn.

Using my knowledge of the geographical make-up of schools in Ghana, I attempted to represent teachers from each lineage affiliation, while also considering the accessibility of the schools to the research assistants administering the surveys. Teachers in Ghana are likely to be teaching in schools located where they reside and thus could be found in schools within their lineage bloc (Gaynor, 1998). The transfer of teachers across lineage divides is not a non-common phenomenon though (Gaynor, 1998; Mulkeen & Dandan, 2008). However, there were, for instance, more Ewe teachers (patrilineals) teaching in their Ewe localities than can be found Akan teachers (matrilineals) within the Ewe localities and the vice versa.

Since each lineage bloc is a confederation of three or more ethnic groups (i.e., ethnic groups), at least one school was selected from each ethnic group. For instance, the matrilineal bloc is a confederation of four major ethnic groups, each with its unique characteristics in their substantive geographic locations with clear linguistic differences. There are the Asantis, Fantes, Brong-Ahafos, and Nzimas that form the matrilineal Akan group. The patrilineal confederation includes the Ewes, Gas, Kokombas, Nanumbas, Walas, and Kusas, *inter alia.*

The data on TTC provided the figures on the proportion of female-headed institutions. Out of the 38 TTCs, seven schools were identified as female-headed. Three out of the seven female-headed TTCs were selected purposefully due to their geographical locations to represent the different lineage affiliations. Judgment sampling again was used to determine which second cycle institutions that were not teacher training colleges and yet were female-headed. Specifically, I used my knowledge of the fact that parochial or mission schools that are unisex and all-female are likely to be female-headed. Once a school was identified from the Catholic almanac, snowball sampling was used in selecting subsequent participating schools. Thus, heads of the first identified institutions referred the researcher to other female-headed schools. Nine schools that were female-headed institutions were selected from those leads based on their location in the lineage blocs. This process resulted in a total of 12 second-cycle schools selected to sample teachers from, six from each lineage bloc.

Power Analysis

A power analysis was conducted to determine the minimum number of participants required in order to detect statistical significance at an alpha level of .05 with a power of at least .80. *Power* is the conditional probability that the null hypothesis will be rejected when the null hypothesis is false (Cohen, 1977). The power was set at .80, which is the minimum acceptable value (Cohen, 1988). The following equation was used to determine the minimum sample size needed (McNeil et al., 1996, p. 169): $N = (L/f^2) + m1$.

Where $L = f^2 \times (N-m1)$, f^2 = effect size, and m1 = number of independent variables in the full model + the unit vector

The following parameters were set:

> alpha level = .05
> f^2 = .15
> predictors = 4
> unit vector = 1
> power = .80

The effect size was set at .15 because this is the minimum value needed to yield a medium/moderate effect size (Cohen, 1988). Using these parameters, L = 11.94 according to the power table provided by McNeil et al. (1996, p. 346). A minimum sample size of 85 teachers was determined:

> $N = (11.94/.15) + (4+1)$
> $N = 85$

Thus, a minimum of 85 teachers needed to be included in the sample in order to detect statistical significance at an alpha level of .05 and a power of .80.

Procedure for Administering Surveys

Data were collected between 2006 - 2009. Prior to conducting the study, Institutional Review Board approval was obtained for piloting the instruments for this study (see Appendix B). I sent the headmistresses in the 12 second-cycle schools a letter requesting permission to recruit teachers from their schools to participate in the survey. The recruitment letter is provided in Appendix C. After obtaining consent from all 12 headmistresses, either the researcher or the field assistants met with the headmistresses in person to confirm their consent and answer any questions regarding the research study. Teachers were identified through the staff list provided for the schools selected for the study. Two time blocs were set for the administration of the questionnaire. The teachers were gathered in the teachers' lounges at their respective schools to complete the surveys. The SRES was administered first. The GSBDS was administered after a 10-minute interval. Teachers were not allowed to talk to colleagues during the survey administration and during the 10-minute interval. It took the teachers approximately 45 minutes to complete the surveys.

The researcher administered the surveys in three of the 12 schools. Two university professors and a headmistress of a junior secondary school in Ghana were recruited to administer the surveys to the teachers in the other nine remaining schools. These field assistants were provided with background information on the study and trained on the protocol of the survey administration. The field assistants were also provided with a script to read to the survey participants (see Appendix D).

The headmistresses were not allowed in or near the teachers' lounges during the survey administration time. This was to minimize the potential of intimidation of the teachers who were presumed to have responded in an atmosphere free of internal or external coercion, intimidation, and or fear of being censured. To maintain the confidentiality of the teachers' responses, unique identification numbers were assigned to the teachers. This was to ensure that no identification information was provided on the surveys except these numbers, which were to match their responses to the SRES and GSBDS questionnaires.

Instrumentation

This section provides a description of the instruments used to collect the data on the independent variables and dependent variable. The Sex-Role Egalitarianism Scale (SRES), developed by King and King (1993), was used to measure teachers' degree of egalitarianism. Teachers' degree of perceived social distance with their headmistress was measured using the Ghana-Specific Behavioral Differential Scale (GSBDS), developed by the researcher. A demographic survey was also used to gather information on the teachers' age, gender, and lineage ties. A description of each instrument including the validity and reliability evidence for each instrument will be addressed in the next section.

Sex-Role Egalitarianism Scale

Instrumentation design. The teachers' gender ideological belief was measured using the Sex-Role Egalitarianism Scale [SRES] (King & King, 1993). There are four versions of the SRES: two 95-item alternate full forms and two 25-item alternate abbreviated forms. This study used one of the full form versions (Form B) of the SRES, which consists of 95 items rated on a 5-point Likert-type scale ranging from "strongly agree" to "strongly disagree." It consists of five domains with 19 items in each domain. The SRES instrument contains statements about attitudes toward women's gender role behaviors and men's gender role behaviors, thus making it suitable for a broader assessment of perspectives on gender-role attitudes in the given Ghanaian context.

The first domain is labeled *marital roles* and asks participants to rate the degree to which they agree with statements regarding the equality or inequality of wives and husbands. The domain addresses the various aspects of their relationships to each other and their home life; this does not include beliefs about their roles as parents. An example item from this domain is, "A marriage is probably happier if the husband has more education than the wife." The second domain is labeled *parental roles* and rates participants' beliefs about the equality or inequality of mothers and fathers regarding issues about the various aspects of their roles as parents. An example item from this domain is, "Mothers and fathers of small children should have an equal right to work outside the home." The third domain, *employment roles,* pertains to participants' beliefs about equality or inequality of females and males regarding issues related to paid employment. An example item of this domain reads, "Women make better receptionists than men do." The fourth domain is labeled, *social-interpersonal-heterosexual roles,* asks participants to rate the degree to which they belief about the equality or inequality of females and males in their relationships to social groups and individuals, and to one another on an interpersonal or sexual basis. An example item from this domain reads, "Women should have as much opportunity to have an evening with the girls as men do with the boys." The fifth and final domain, labeled *educational roles,* asks participants to rate the degree to which their beliefs are about the equality or inequality of males and females in school, university, or training facility setting, including roles as students or providers of education and training. An example item from this domain is, "It is more rewarding to teach girls than to teach boys."

King and King (1993) found that a single factor solution was optimal for all forms (B, K, BB, and KK) indicating that each of the four forms yielded a single factor measuring one single construct (degree of egalitarianism). Items scores are assigned such that a score of 5 represents the most egalitarian position while a score of 1 represents the least egalitarian (traditional) position (King & King, 1993). Total domain scores will be obtained by summing the participants' ratings of all 95 items to yield a composite score ranging from 95-475. The higher the score on the SRES, the more egalitarian the teacher is. The lower the score on the SRES, the less egalitarian is the teacher.

Reliability evidence. The SRES has consistently yielded acceptable reliability indices (Beere et al., 1984; Cammarata, 1986; Honeck, 1981;

Katenbrink, 2006; King & King, 1993,1997; McGhee, Johnson, & Liverpool, 2002; McHugh & Frieze, 1997; Roaboteg-Saric & Ravlic, 1990; Rubini & Antoneli, 1986; Scandura, Tejeda, &Lankua, 1995; Ui & Matsui, 2008). The internal consistency of the scores has been found to range from .70 to .97 (Beere et al., 1984; Katenbrink, 2006: King & King, 1993). Beere et al. (1984) analyzed responses from 530 students and employees from community organizations. The sample consisted of 26% males and 74% females ranging from 18 to 72 year-olds. The internal consistency yielded .97 for total scores and a mean of .87 across the five domains. Katenbrink (2006) also estimated the internal consistency of a German translated version of the SRES administered to 379 participants including 250 women and 129 men ranging from 18 to 65 years old. The Cronbach's alpha reliability coefficient for total score was .96 and the mean internal consistency across all five domains yielded .82.

The test-retest reliability of the scores produced from the SRES was also found to be high, in the .90 range (Beere et al., 1984; King & King, 1993). The test-retest reliability coefficient yielded a total score values of .88 and .91 with a mean of .85 across the five domains (Beere et al., 1984). Beere et al. administered the SRES Forms B and K to a homogeneous sample of 367 police officers, senior citizens, and college students consisting of 56% percent females and 44% males ranging from 18 to 87 years old.

Finally, there is supportive evidence for the reliability of the scores produced from the alternative forms created for the SRES. In a study by King, Beere, King, and Beere, (1984), two forms of the SRES were developed and administered to 367 persons to test the psychometric characteristics of the scale. Forms B and K were administered to the respondents on the same occasion. The respondents included police officers, senior citizens, business undergraduates, and psychology undergraduates. Reliability estimates for domain and total scores ranged from .81 to .97. Their findings also reveal a high coefficient of .93 for the correlation between the two forms. The mean coefficient for the domains was .86. King and King (1997) later replicated the test for all versions of the full and short forms: two 25-item abbreviated and the two alternate 95-item full forms. This replicated study derived reliability indices from a classical test-theory approach, multifaceted generalizability procedures, and an item-response theory based analysis, all of which supported the consistency of the scale measuring what it purports to be measuring.

Evidence from the above studies demonstrates that the SRES has the ability of showing a high degree of reliability overtime, regardless of the culture and the context of the respondents.

Validity evidence. A study by Katenbrink (2006) yields support for the unidimentionality of the SRES scale. The point for unidimensionality of the scale was established using principal axis factor analysis. The computed coefficient of congruence between factor structures for all respondents was f = 999. Katenbrink (2006) further analyzed the single subscales (marital roles, parental roles, employment roles, social-interpersonal-heterosexual roles, and educational roles) with product moment correlations. Results indicated significant positive correlations with five among the domains ranging from .72 to .84. This respectable range implies that the domains do not stand as orthogonal subscales but together, the entire subscales measure one construct (the degree of egalitarianism).

Some studies have found evidence of convergent and divergent validity for scores generated by the SRES. Researchers tested the theoretical framework of the SRES with other measures of gender role attitudes to see if their constructs corresponded to each other's (Honeck, 1981; Jaffa, 1985; King & King, 1997; King, et al., 1984). These studies tested the congruity of SRES with the Attitudes Toward Women Scale (AWS; Spence & Helmreich, 1972 and MacDonald Sex Role Survey, MacDonald, 1974) and found correlations ranging from .60 to .86. Jaffa (1985) correlated scores on Form B of the SRES with scores on the AWS using college students. Both instruments assess traditional and non-traditional views of gender roles and yielded a strong positive correlation of 86 (Jaffa, 1985). Honeck (1981) correlated Forms B and K of the SRES with scores on two other gender-role measures – the Attitudes Toward Women Scale (AWS) and the MacDonald Sex Role Survey (MacDonald, 1974). Using high school and college students as the study sample, correlations range from .60 to .80. In a similar study by King et al. (1994), scores from students on the SRES Form B were shown to share a linear relationship (r = .88) with scores on the MacDonald Sex Role Survey.

King and King (1997) reviewed studies providing discriminant validity evidence for the SRES. These studies included the works of Beere et al. (1984), King and King (1991), King et al. (1994), and Stith (1986). In the study of Beere et al. (1984), a sub-sample of 160 out of 367 participants completed the Edwards Social Desirability Scale (ESDS; Edwards, 1957) with the Forms B and K of the SRES. The study derived preliminary evidence of nomological validity (expected differences between women versus men) from the confirmation of two *a priori* hypotheses: Women reported higher degree of egalitarianism than men, and psychology students scored more egalitarian than business students and both student groups scored more egalitarian than senior citizens and police officers.

The total domain correlation scores between the SRES and the desirability index were relatively low, supporting the degree of discriminant validity. The correlation between social desirability and SRES scores ranged from -0.03 to +0.18. The ESDS correlation with the B and K were .17 and .09, respectively. Domain scores range from .14 to .19 for Form B and -.03 to .18 for Form K. In another study, Stith (1986) correlated scores on the short Form BB of the SRES with scores on the Marlowe-Crowne Social Desirability Scale (MCSDS, Crone & Marlowe, 1964) using a sample of police officers and found no significant correlation, with a coefficient of -.14.

Further discriminant validity evidence was established by King and King (1990) who correlated scores of college students on SRES B and K with scores on the Bem Sex Role Inventory (Bem, 1974). Correlation for discriminant validity was insignificant with resulting coefficients ranging from .07 to .15. In another study by King et al. (1994), score of college students on the SRES B discriminated with scores on the Personal Attributes Questionnaire (Spence et al., 1974). The two domains subscale tested for this study included Feminity/Expressiveness and Masculinity/Instrumentality. The resulting correlation of .21 for the Feminity/Expressiveness subscale and .08 for the Masculinity/Instrumentality domain were found.

The implication of the insignificant correlations reported in the studies above with negative to low correlation coefficients indicate that scores on the SRES were less likely to have been biased by social desirability conditions. In other words, that the respondent most likely answered the items truthfully according to how they felt and were not likely influenced by the social environment.

Ghanaian Specific Behavioral Differential Scale

Development of the Modified GSBDS. The Ghanaian Specific Behavioral Differential Scale (GSBDS) was used to measure the criterion variable – degree of social distance. This instrument is a modified version of Triandis' (1971) Behavioral Differential Scale [See Appendix E for Tiandis' scale]. The instrument was modified to suitably address contextual indices of behavioral intensions within the Ghanaian culture. Modifications were done of five survey items of the GSBDS from its original rendering by replacing the item wording with meaningful words and phrases used in the Ghanaian culture to express one's attitude towards one's stimulus person. To these five modified items, five new items were added, yielding a total of 10 items. The instrument uses phrases such as, *feeling comfortable taking her orders; vote her into a political office; support her promotion,* among others, referring to females in authority positions; positions which are usually associated with male figures. For example, some of the semantics used by Triandis in constructing the original measure, of which this modification was made, took into account the North American culture and population. For the modified version, this study took account of the Ghanaian socio-cultural context

Triandis used phrases like, "I would exclude this person from my neighborhood." The import of such a semantic indicates hatred for the out-group. Yet social distance is not necessarily a function of hate; even though hatred could as well evoke such a behavioral response. The social context addressed by this revised scale (GSBDS) is the sub-Saharan Ghanaian culture. Certainly, the gender discrimination in the Ghanaian context is not a function of hate. It has to do with conflict with deep-seated gender role expectations that favor men with superior statuses and women with subordinate statuses. Hence, culturally relevant words must be used to test appropriate social distance responses of teacher. Consequently, Triandis' *exclusion from neighborhood* item would not be meaningful or useful in the Ghanaian context and was thus avoided.

The construction of the 10-item GSBDS went through various stages of evaluation and analysis. First, a content validation of the instrument (GSBDS) was done by five carefully selected technical individuals. These individual judges were given the preliminary draft of the GSBDS instrument, a Questionnaire Development Matrix (Appendix F) and an Instrument Evaluation Matrix (IEM) that provided operational definitions for each of the items on the instrument. The judges were to study and critique the structure, contents, and intent of the scale, and to give their responses on the IEM provided them (see Appendix G). Their task was to correct, change parts of items, or rewrite entire items. They were allowed to rearrange, or remove an item depending on whether or not they judged that item as appropriately measuring the construct, *social distance.* Their comments and suggestions were either to be written on the IEM or on a separate sheet of paper for the researcher's review.

The items given to the judges for this assignment also included the instructions for the field assistants that were to be read to the participants during the survey itself and also the letter of consent, which was sent to the headmistresses of the participating schools. The instruction to be read to the participants addressed two things. The first part explained the intent of the survey and its ethical considerations. The second part explained how participants should answer the specific questions. All of the above materials were prefixed by a short summary of the survey itself. This summary explained what the selected judges for this exercise should pay attention to while evaluating the items: what the literature says, and what they were expected to do as judges. Thus, all of this information served to guide the judges in their evaluation of the GSBDS instrument.

Table 11 show the five judges selected for the instrument evaluation and their countries of origin. Judges were selected, some, based on their expertise in and familiarity with the construct of social distance, others, based on their knowledge in scale construction and or familiarity with the nuances of the sub-Saharan Ghanaian culture. Judges included four males and one female. Four judges were Ghanaians and one judge was an

American. Three of the selected judges were university professors teaching Research methods, Economics, and Sociology at the time of the exercise. The remaining two judges (all Ghanaians) were a research analyst and a physician. All of them were given the same materials for the evaluation exercise. Further modifications were made to the GSBDS based on the comments and recommendations of the judges. An expert researcher and statistician with a long history of scholarly publication evaluated the face validity of the GSBDS before it was content analyzed by the judges.

Table 11. *Selected Judges for Content Validation*

Judges' Country of Origin	Professional Expertise and Country of Residence
USA	Professor Emeritus, Statistician and Researcher, USA
Ghana	Professor of Sociology & Director of Pan-African Studies, USA
Ghana	Director: Research Analyst, Grand Rapids, MI, USA
Ghana	Professor of Economics (Demography) University of Cape Coast, Ghana
Ghana	Physician, Pediatric Resident, Akron Children's Hospital, USA

Semantic import and item relevancy. The operational definitions and the semantic import of the items chosen for the GSBDS scale reverberate with the Ghanaian socio-cultural nuance and express individual's personal behavioral disposition underlying that individual's relational attitude. The items on the modified scale were operationally defined.

The first item reads *I would/would not admire her ideas.* Admiring or not admiring a person's ideas stems from personal misgivings on the part of the actor about the credibility of the person of interest. Holding a person in high esteem makes her/his ideas admirable and having a poor image of a person makes her/his ideas worthless and non-admirable (Blumer, 1937) to the beholder.

The second item reads *I am/I am not comfortable taking directives from her.* A person, who feels uncomfortable taking orders from a woman supervisor, if not for any personal misgivings, is most likely expressing some aversion towards female authority. Such a person will most likely relate poorly to that female authority on a social level, at least. There is a complex here underlying the observer's feelings. Either he or she feels that his or her dignity is being compromised or being challenged to disrepute by the female boss or because he or she sees the female superior as an underdog wielding power unconventionally (Skrla, Reyes, & Scheurich, 2000). Such a feeling is indicative of a disposition that will evoke social distance.

The third item, which states *I would/ I would not admire her character,* is a natural projection of the second item, *I am/I am not comfortable taking directives from her.* Admiring a person's character is according that person some recognition, respect, and credit for the qualities that that person possesses and exhibits (Oduro & Macbeath, 2003; Triandis, 1971). A person who expresses such views in the negative towards a female superior is rejecting the very epitome of the authority the female superior is and exercises. Respecting *her character,* however, also acknowledges her authority as befitting her dignity and the respect that goes with her office as a boss. She is therefore respected for who she is because her character is admirable. A person with such feelings about a stimulus person is likely to endear him/herself to that stimulus person.

The fourth item, *I would/I would not vote her into a political office,* as the above items, expresses a person's rejection or acceptance of the female superior's qualifying credentials. In Ghana, as in much of West African sub-region, people are voted into political positions based on how well liked they are by their constituents. Stating one's intention as not willing to vote for an individual reveals a degree of dislike for that person. Giving a person a-no-vote is declaring one's rejection of that person's competence to assume leadership position. In a sense, it connotes the denial of the candidate's ability to lead (Mostafa, 2005). Interpersonal relationship with such a stimulus person is not likely by the one who is rejecting her or unwilling to vote for her.

The fifth item reads *I would/I would not gossip with her.* Ghanaians will gossip with close acquaintances, people they can trust or people with whom they share common social grounds. In other words, people gossip with individuals who share their opinions and beliefs, people with whom they identify and feel comfortable, and people they hold trustworthy. Declaring one's intention not to gossip with a person suggests some distrust for that person and seeing him/her as not deserving intimate interaction, (Jalava, 2003).

The sixth item, *I would/I would not accept her as an intimate friend,* flows naturally from the fifth item. A level of acceptance or aversion is being expressed here. If you cannot accept a person as an intimate friend, for instance, then you have at least some hidden discriminatory tendencies towards that person. With such expressed intent, there is no room for a common ground for social affinity (Ofei-Aboagye, 1994; Osmond & Thorn, 1993; Sugarman & Frankel, 1987). Interpersonal relationship with such a person is not likely.

The seventh item states, *I would/I would not support her promotion.* You must have faith in and or an appreciation of a person's performance to support his/her promotion. Being unwilling to support her promotion may suggest two things: the lack of confidence in the person's ability or an unfounded dislike for that individual (Bogardus, 1959). If one cannot support a person's promotion, either because of personal dislike or the lack of confidence in that person then it is not likely to see close social distance between those two individuals.

The eighth item, *I would/I would not confide my secrets in her,* again expresses a person's declared intention to or not to share common ground with or enter into any close social ties with the stimulus person. Such expressed feelings in the negative are the corollaries of a lack of trust and disrespect for the person's integrity (Blunner, 1937; Triandis & Gelfand, 1998).

The ninth item reads *I would/ would not defend her rights if they were jeopardized.* Nothing is more accepting or rejecting of a person than this statement. The refusal to protect a person from being hurt physically or emotionally is an act of hatred or dislike for that person. It is a callous indifference to the plight of that person, mostly done out of hatred (Triandis & Triandis, 1988). Anybody who expresses such a view in the negative about another will most likely distance him/herself from that person.

The last item reads *I would/would not have her as my mentor*. Acceptance of a person as one's mentor is an endorsement of that person's capabilities and abilities to mentor. A rejection of a person's mentorship may indicate a doubt of that person's ability or capabilities to be a mentor on the part of the to-be-mentored. It may also be indicative of personal dislike for the mentor-to-be because of some probable discriminatory tendencies (Buchan & Croson, 2004; Jalava, 2003). Such stated intent suggests the degree of social distance a person is willing to or not willing to dare with one's stimulus person.

The numbering on the GSBDS is also one of the modifications made of the original Triandis' Social Distance (SD) Scale. On Triandis' SD scale, items ranges were not numbered. The numbering of item ranges on the GSBDS is to give to the respondents a visual value of their stated intent.

The expert-judges indicated whether items on the scale were congruent with the construct being measured. Appendix H illustrates the verdict of the judges. The check marks and the crosses, which were later recoded for easy computation of scores, respectively indicated affirmation or rejection of items' validity. The checks were coded as "1" indicating affirmation and the crosses were coded as "0" indicating rejection. The task of the expert-judges was to accept or reject an item as measuring social distance construct.

A congruency table rated the verdicts of the expert-judges about the validity of scale items in percentages indicating the strength of agreement on each test item's validity. Thus, while two of the judges estimated the strength of validity at 80% each, three of the judges rated it at 100%. The average congruency percentage (ACP), which is the index value of the overall percentage scores of the experts-judges, revealed that the strength of validity for the test stands at 92%. According to Popham (1978), Waltz, Strickland, and Lenz (2005), and Polit and Beck (2006), a congruency of 90% and above should be accepted as a satisfactory level for validity estimate for a scale. Hence, the ACP of 92% for the modified GSBDS provided support for the content validity of the items.

The Final modified GSBDS. The GSBDS measures behavioral intention of the willingness or non-willingness to trade social space or do certain things for or with one's stimulus person (headmistresses in this case). There are ten items on the modified GSBDS rated on a 6-point scale ranging from 1 "I would" to 6 "I would not." Lower scores indicate less social distance (greater willingness to associate with the female head) while higher scores indicate greater social distance (less willingness to associate with the female head).

Total scores on the GSBDS are computed by summing up participants' ratings to yield a total composite score ranging from 10 to 60. Lower scores represent less perceived social distance and higher scores representing greater perceived social distance between teachers and their headmistresses.

Reliability and Validity Evidence for the GSBDS

Reliability evidence. The internal consistency and test-retest reliability were computed using a sample of teachers from the target population. To test the internal consistency of the survey, an inter-item correlation was done using data from a target population of teachers from a female-headed institution in Ghana. The internal consistency reliability estimate for Cronbach's alpha was .89. The item-total correlations are provided in Table 12. The item-total correlation is the correlation of each item with the combined effects of all items on the survey. The inter-item correlations show the mean correlation of each item with every other item in the survey. In other words, the values show the correlation between each item and the average of the other items on the survey.

The *Alpha if Item Deleted* shows what the alpha will be if the particular item is deleted from the survey. As seen in Table 12, removing item 5, "I would/would not gossip with her," would increase the internal consistency by .01. This value is insignificant and thus this item was not dropped. Also, in the qualitative assessment of the judges, item 5 received 60% approval indicating that the item should be retained among the other items as measuring the construct of social distance.

Table 12. *Internal Consistency for Items on the GSBDS*

Item	Correlated Item-Total Correlation	Cronbach's Alpha if Item Deleted	
1	.831	.867	
2	.647	.880	
3	.663	.878	
4	.745	.871	
5	.296	.897	
6	.525	.889	
7	.642	.879	
8	.722	.873	
9	.622	.881	
10	.635	.879	

To further test the internal consistency of the survey, a split-halves analysis was conducted. The GSBDS survey was administered to teachers drawn from a second cycle institution headed by a headmistress. The scale of 10 items was then divided into two halves (odd-numbered items against even-numbered items). The correlation between forms was .87. The Spearman-Brown coefficient was .93 and the Guttman split-half coefficient was .92 (see Table 13).

Table 13. *Split-half Reliability Results for the GSBDS*

	Split A	Split B
Correlated Item-Total Correlation	.868	.868
Squared Multiple Correlation	.754	.754
Correlation between Forms		.868
Spearman-Brown Coefficient		.929
Guttman Split-Half Coefficient		.918

A test-retest reliability test was also computed for the GSBDS with responses of teachers from the target population in Ghana. The teachers completed the GSBDS survey at Time 1 and then Time 2 two weeks later. The test-retest reliability was .89, indicating that the ranking of the scores produced from the survey was consistent over time.

Generally a coefficient of .88 is acceptable for scale reliability (DeCoster & Claypool, 2004). The coefficient for each of the reliability test for the GSBDS yielded coefficients of .89, .92, and .89 for the test-retest, split-halves, and internal consistency reliability tests, respectively.

Validity evidence. Content validation of the GSBDS was estimated from the assessment of expert-judges. There are two types of face validity as identified by Newman et al. (2006). The first involves the assessment of the item validity by a group of chosen students or subjects experts who give a face-value judgment of whether the scale appears to be measuring what it is intended to measure. This type of validation, of course, is perfunctory and is the least accurate of face validity (Newman et al., 2006). The second, more sophisticated approach, involves expert-judges' assessment and evaluation of all items on the scale to see if they actually measure the construct they purport to be measuring. This latter approach is called expert-judge validity or content experts' validity (Newman et al., 2006). Both methods were adopted in this study for the GSBDS as discussed earlier above.

To further ascertain that the GSBDS truly measures what it is purported to measure (social distance), a Principal Component Analysis (PCA) was conducted to examine the underlying structure of the GSBDS scale before the analysis (see Chapter IV for detail discussion of factor analysis of the scale). Two factors emerged indicating that the social distance construct is comprised of two orthogonal domains. These domains are named as *Accommodative Disposition Domain* and *Interpersonal Affective Disposition Domain*. Consequently, these two factors were treated as separate dependent variables in this study.

The *Accommodative Disposition Domain* encases attitudes of acceptance and accommodation expressed by the items that loaded on it. The import of these items exudes feelings of personal trust in and acceptance of one's stimulus person (in this study, the headmistress). Admiring a person's ideas and feeling comfortable taking his/her orders or to admire his/her character, to defend his/her rights, to support his/her promotion, and to accept him/her as one's mentor all of these do reveal a sense of trust, likeness, support, and the willingness to accept and accommodate the authority and opinion of that stimulus person. These items were on the first domain.

The second domain, the *Interpersonal Affective Disposition Domain* captures the sense of readiness to enter into a relationship with the stimulus person. This is because the abstractions expressed in the items under this domain (see Chapter IV under Scale Analysis) operationalize the willingness for interpersonal relationship with the stimulus person; hence, the name interpersonal affective disposition domain. Consequently, these two domains (accommodative disposition and interpersonal affective disposition) will now be treated as the two domains of the dependent variable of the study.

Data Analyses

This section discusses the conceptual models of the variables explored, the assumptions to be tested, and the methods used in screening the research data for main analysis. All data analyses were conducted using SPSS version 19.0. The factor analysis results showed that perceived social distance did not form a single factor (see Chapter IV). As a result of this finding, two simultaneous multiple regressions were used to address research questions 1 and 2. This study is an exploratory study in that no specific model was being tested prior to this study. There is no prior literature examining the relationship between these independent variables and social distance. Thus, simultaneous multiple regressions were used whereby the independent variables were entered in a single block as illustrated in Figure 2 (Tabachnick & Fidell, 2001). Degree of egalitarianism, lineage affiliation, gender, and age were entered as the independent variables. Teachers' degree of perceived social distance defined as accommodative disposition and interpersonal affective disposition with their headmistresses were the criterion variables. The categorical variables (gender and lineage tie) were dummy coded where male = 0 and female = 1 for the gender variable and patrilineal = 0 and matrilineal = 1 for the lineage tie variable.

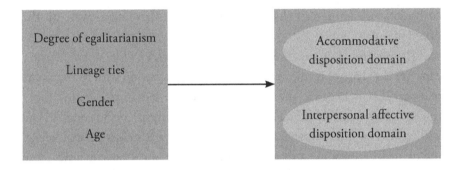

Figure 2. *Variables' profile for multiple regression after independent variable (SD) was factor analyzed*

The model for each multiple regression is expressed as: $y = \beta_0 + \beta_1 X_1 + \beta_2 X_2 + \beta_3 X3 + \beta 4X4 + E$. The intent of the researcher is to estimate the $\beta o, \beta 1, \beta 2, \beta 3, \beta 4$ by obtaining $\hat{y} = b_{o + b1\,X1} + b_{2X2} + b_{3\,X3} + b_{4X4,}$ where $\hat{y}$ is the predicted value on the *dependent variable,* b_o is the y intercept (which is the value of y when all the *X* values are zero), Xs represent each independent variable and the *b*'s are the regression coefficients or beta weights that determine which set of the observed independent variables (IVs) shows the strongest influence on the criterion variable. The higher the beta values the stronger the influence of the independent variable on the dependent variable. Another way to represent this to see how the simultaneous regression could be performed based on the regression models is:

$$y = \beta_0 + \beta_1 X_1 + \varepsilon . = \text{Lineage system}$$
$$y = \beta_0 + \beta_2 X_2 + \varepsilon . = \text{Degree of egalitarianism}$$
$$y = \beta_0 + \beta_3 X_3 + \varepsilon . = \text{Age}$$
$$y = \beta_0 + \beta_4 X_4 + \varepsilon . = \text{Gender}$$

Testing of Assumptions

The following assumptions were tested prior to conducting the multiple regression: ratio of cases-to-IVs, normality, collinearity, linearity, and homoscedasticity (Tabacnick & Fidell, 2001). These assumptions were factored into the series of considerations for the use of this model. The testing of these assumptions is necessary when doing simultaneous multiple regressions (Tabacnick & Fidell, 2001).

Ratio of Cases to Independent Variables

The ratio of case-to-independent variables concerns the number of cases required for a sample size for the regression to be meaningful. According to Tabachnick and Fidell (2001), finding this ratio "depends on a number of issues, including the desired power, alpha level, number of predictors, and expected effect sizes" (p. 117). The minimum ratio of valid cases to independent variables for MR is 5 to 1. There are other recommendations for adopting which procedure helps in determining the number of cases needed when testing for multiple correlation and when testing for each independent variable within the set (Tabachnick & Fidell, 2001). This study matched the number of cases to the independent variables of the study using specific computation methods appropriate for multiple regression [$N \geq 50 + 8m$ and $N \geq 104 + m$] (Tabachnick & Fidell, 2001).

Collinearity

Multiple regression models have the potential of incurring the problem of multicollinearity. Multicollinearity occurs when the independent variables in the analysis are too highly correlated. Multicollinearity is detected when there is no statistical significance in any of the t-ratios for the individual coefficients (when several IVs are involved), and yet the overall F is statistically significant. The standard errors of the coefficients are increased with the presence of multicollinearity, which can cause an otherwise significant coefficient not to be significant. The first goal of this study is simply to predict our two dependent variables (accommodative disposition domain and the interpersonal affective disposition domain variables) from a set of independent variables (lineage system, degree of egalitarianism, age, and gender). In this case, then, multicollinearity is not as much of a concern because the R^2 will show how well the models influence (predict) the values of the dependent variables. The second objective of this study is to assess the impact of the various independent variables (Xs) on the dependent variables (Ys), which is where the problem of multicollinearity may arise.

The Variance Inflation Factor (VIF) was computed to determine how much the variances of the estimated coefficients are increased when there is no correlation among the independent variables. According to Tabachnick and Fidell (2001), a VIF of 5.0 and above for any one of the independent variables indicates the presence of multicollinearity and was the criterion used in this study.

Normality and Multivariate Outliers

The continuous level variables must be normally distributed in a multiple regression. Variables that are not normally distributed (highly skewed or kurtotic) have the potential of distorting relationship and significance tests (Osborne & Waters, 2002; Pena & Prieto, 2001; Tabachnick & Fidell, 2001). Outliers are abnormal deviations of data from normal data variability. It is noted by scholars that multivariate measures have the intrinsic characteristic of possibly experiencing changes during the process of analysis thereby generating clusters of outliers (Filzmoser, Reimann, & Garrett, 2003; Pena & Prieto, 2001). This distortion renders meaningless the values of the location and parameters of data variability. The assumption of normality was tested in four ways as outlined next.

First, *Mahalanobis Distance* was computed to detect multivariate outliers. Mahalanobis Distance calculates the distance of scores of individual cases from the center cluster of remaining cases using the

Chi-square statistic (Tabachnick & Fidell, 2001). A Chi-square value exceeding the critical value associated with an alpha level of .001 indicates a significant multivariate outlier (Mertler & Vannatta, 2010). A Chi-square critical value of 18.47 was associated with an alpha level of .001 with four degrees of freedom and was the criterion used in this study.

Second, a visual inspection of the scatterplot matrices was conducted as recommended by Tabachnick and Fidell (2001) to detect univariate, bi-variate, and potential multivariate outliers. Also, Z-standardized scores were computed for the continuous level variables to test if significant outliers existed.

Third, the skewness and kurtosis of the continuous variables were computed. Skewness refers to an abnormal distribution of scores where most of the scores in the distribution are on one side showing an asymmetrical distribution. Skewness indicates a deviation from the normal curve and could either be positive (deviation to the right) or negative (deviation to the left). Kurtosis refers to the height of the distribution curve. Acceptable values for skewness and kurtosis range from -1.0 to +1.0 (Meyers et al., 2006), the criterion used in this study.

Fourth, a Shapiro-Wilk test was conducted to further test the multivariate normality assumption. The Shapiro-Wilk test is said to be one of the most powerful test in detecting outliers or deviations from normality (Stevens, 1996). According to Stevens (2002), acceptable *p*-values should be greater than .001. This was the criterion used in this study.

Linearity

Linearity must also be met when conducting correlational analyses. The predictor variables and criterion variables are assumed to share a linear relationship. If a non-linear relationship exists between a predictor and criterion variable, then residual results will be an under-estimation of the true relationship, thus, increasing the Type II error for IV and Type I error (Meyers et al., 2006). Linearity was tested by conducting a visual inspection of the standardized residuals plotted against the predicted values (Meyers et al., 2006; Tabachnick & Fidell, 2001).

Homoscedasticity

Homoscedasticity is the assumption that the dependent variable exhibits a similar amount of variance across the range of values for an independent variable (Tabachnick & Fidell, 2001). In other words, when there is homogeneity in the variance of errors across all levels of the independent variables, homoscedasticity is met. However, in some cases, variance errors may differ in value at different levels of a given independent variable. When this happens, heteroscedasticity is said to have occurred. Even though the effect of heteroscedasticity on significance tests is negligible (Tabachnick & Fidell, 2002), its presence can lead to serious distortion of interpretation of the research findings, thereby increasing the probability of Type I error (Osborne & Walters, 2002).

According to Tabachnick and Fidell (2002), the assumptions of normality and homoscedasticity are related. Consequently, normality in multivariate distribution indicates homoscedasticity. The practical implication of homoscedasticity for regression for instance is that the increase in the error of prediction is associated with the increase in the size of prediction. In other words, as error of prediction increases, the size of prediction also increases.

Tabachnick and Fidell (2002) suggest avoiding the interaction of two independent variables when one is not a part of the regression equation. These suggestions were utilized in this study to check this assumption.

Limitations

Threats to internal and external validity exist in this study. Internal validity refers to the degree to which the researcher can confidently and accurately state that the obtained results of a study are a function of the variables measured in the study and not by any other unintended factor. In other words, that the changes in the dependent variable can be explained by the effect of the independent variable(s). In a non-randomized sample, findings could be inaccurate (Newman et al., 2006). Since a non-experimental design was used in this study, causal inferences cannot be made between the independent and dependent variables (Gall et al., 2010; Meyers & Gamst, 2006). Potential threats to internal validity in this study, therefore, are confounding variables, response bias, and measurement error, which will be treated in the next section. External validity, however, refers to the ability to generalize findings of the study to the general population that could not be tested. In other words, it is the ability to say that the behavior of a study sample is true for the general population. Potential threat to external validity in this study is population validity. These probable threats are discussed in the next section.

Threats to Internal Validity

Confounding variables. Extraneous variables changing systematically along with any of the independent variables could distort the accurate interpretation of the variance explained in the dependent variable. Extraneous variables refer to factors other than the independent variables examined in the study that might explain the variance in the dependent variable (Gall et al., 2010). There may be additional factors not investigated in this study that may explain the variance in the teachers' perceived social distance with their headmistress. Such probable variables could include, but are not limited to, school climate, teachers' socio-economic status, and teachers' job satisfaction.

Response bias. One of the research assistants used for the administration of the questionnaires was a female school principal. Even though this research assistant conducted surveys in schools other than hers, her status as female head may intimidate any participant who recognized her as such. Since the questionnaire for the dependent variable concerns favorable and or unfavorable attitudes from valued opinions of teachers about female school heads, it should be noted that participants' responses could be affected by the presence of another female school head who may be recognized as such by the participants, whether or not she is the head of that institution.

Measurement error. The use of the GSBDS to measure the criterion variable is with caution, given the fact that this is the first time the newly constructed scale is being used in a study. Even though the GSBDS is modeled on the universally accepted model used by Triandis (1965) and Bogardus (1959), and many other scholars, the modifications made of this scale have only been tested in a pilot study. The reliability of the scores produced from the GSBDS has not yet been tested with a large sample. According to Popham (1978), there always exists a margin of subjectivity in determining validity of the inferences drawn from a measure using human experts. The reliability and validity estimates for the scale were determined only during the construction of the scale through the pilot study. This notwithstanding, the reliability issues for the GSBDS have been confidently addressed in this study and factor analysis has also been conducted prior to the main analyses of the study (see Chapter IV).

Threats to External Validity

Population validity. A population validity threat exists in this study in that the findings from this study might not be generalizable to the target population of interest (Meyers & Gamst, 2006). First, a non-probability sampling method was used, which will not generally represent the general Ghanaian teacher population. Consequently, this researcher will refrain from making causal inferences and generalization of results to the target population. In spite of all the standard cautions taken by the researcher, the threat to external validity is however likely. This threat may be due to the assumption by which the target population for this study is conceptualized. This approach was necessary because of the absence of available data on specific population characteristics (see Sampling Method, par. 2). The lack of available data on the target population left the researcher with no other option but to do estimations based on ancillary data from other sectors to assume the population characteristics of the gender balance within school management sector in Ghana. Such estimates are acquiescent to population errors and could threaten the degree of external validity of the results to a target population.

Summary

This chapter summarized the research methodologies used within the corpus of the study. First, it gave a description of the research design (a non-experimental multivariate correlational research) used in this study and discussed the limitations of this design. The derivation of the specific hypotheses was based on findings in the literature review. Participants in the study were chosen from selected second cycle institutions that represent, geographically, the two lineage systems of Ghana. All subjects answered the same survey measuring their degree of egalitarian beliefs and another to determine their degree of social distance with their headmistresses. The instruments used in the survey were the SRES scale and the modified GSBDS.

CHAPTER IV

RESULTS

In this chapter, the data analyses and results are reported. There are three sections to this chapter. The first section reports the descriptive statistics of the study sample and data screening results. The second section presents the reliability analyses on the SRES and GSBDS, factor analysis on the GSBDS, and testing of the assumptions for multiple regressions. In the third section, the results of the correlational analyses and simultaneous multiple regression testing the two main research questions are reported.

Sample

The data used for this study is a primary data collected of teachers in 12 selected schools in Ghana. Of the 398 respondents, 324 participated out of which 10 questionnaires were unusable. This resulted in a total sample size of 314 teachers used in this study. The study data set, therefore, has an acceptable 81.4% response rate and a data present rate of 78.9% (314/398 = .78.89), which exceeds the minimum requirement of 50% data present rate (Langer, 2003). The participants included 174 (55.4%) males and 140 (44.6%) females. The median age was 36 years (SD = 10.94 years). The gender distribution of the sample is confirmatory of the earlier findings from the literature that more men than women are at the higher levels of the academic ladder (Stephens, 2000; Sutherland-Addy, 2002).

A total of 52.9% of the participants reported their lineage descent as patrilineal while 47.1% identified themselves as matrilineal. Even though equal numbers of schools were chosen from each lineage bloc (six each) from which the participants were sampled, the patrilineal respondents were 5.8% margin more than the matrilineal respondents. This distribution is reflective of the general proportion of the distribution of the lineage ties in Ghana (Kannae, 1993).

Data Screening

First, a factor analysis was conducted for the GSBDS scale that measures the social distance (SOCDIS) variable to make determination from the factor loadings. The following data screening methods were employed to check for the potential presence of data entry errors: ratio of Cases to IVs, multivariate outliers, multicollinearity, non-normal distribution of data, non-linearity, and homoscedasticity.

Factor Analysis of Scales

The GSBDS and SRES were considered for factor analysis. Consideration for factor analysis for the two scales (GSBDS and SRES) were based on the recommendation of Tabachnick and Fidell (2001) that there should be at least 5 to 10 cases to a scale item for a variable to qualify for factor analysis. The SRES failed to meet this criterion since the measurement consists of 95 items and the N for this study is 314. Factor analysis could therefore not be conducted on the SRES. This researcher, therefore, followed the convention in the literature using the measure and computed a composite score for SRES scale.

The GSBDS, however, met the criterion and was factor analyzed. A Principal Component Analysis (PCA) was employed using a varimax rotation. Table I1 in Appendix I shows that the measure does not form a unidimensional factor. Two orthogonal factors emerged from this initial run. Initial eigenvalues loading for Factor 1 was 4.565 representing 46% of the variance explained while Factor 2 has 1.534 eigenvalues loading accounting for 15.3% of variance. Both of the factors accounted for about 61% of total the variance explained by all the 10 factors. The scree plot and the pie charts in Appendix I (see Figures I1, I2, I3, and I4 also) illustrate that two factors emerged from the PCA.

Six items loaded on Factor 1 with acceptable values ranging from .686 to .780. These items include items 1-*I would/would not admire her ideas*, item 2-*I am/am not comfortable taking orders from her*, item 3-*I would/would not admire her character*, item 7-*I would/would not support her promotion*, item 9-*I would/would not defend her rights if they were jeopardized*, and item10-*I would/would not have her as my mentor*.

Factor 2 has three items loading on it with values within the acceptable range of .652 to .737. The three items loading meet the minimum criterion of the independent variable (Costello & Osborne, 2005; Tabachnick & Fidell, 2001) to stand as a factor. The items loading on the second factor included item-4 *I would/would not vote her into a political office*, item-6 *I would/would not accept as an intimate friend*, and item-8 *I would/would not confide my secrets in her*.

Two scales then were created from the result of the factor loadings. The creation of scales was guided by the scree plot (see Appendix I) generated by the factor loadings (see Figure I5.). The scree plot is a bi-coordinate plane that plots eigenvalues. Its function here is to select the number of factors to be rotated to final solution for easy interpretation of the subscales (Bryman & Cramer, 2009). Eigenvalues are proportion of variance accounted for by the variables on each factor. As a rule of thumb, a cutoff of 1.0 eigenvalue and above, indicate a strong enough intercorrelation among items for factor extraction (Bryman & Cramer, 2009; Tabachnick & Fidell, 2001). In Figure I1 (Appendix I), only two factors fall above the trajectory point of disjunction. Anything below 1.0 was rejected.

Item 5, *I would/would not gossip with her*, cross-loaded on both factors and was dropped because of its ambiguous communality values (see Table 14). According to Costello and Osborne (2005), a cross-loader indicates a poorly written item or a possibly flawed *a priori* factor structure. Item 5 cross-loaded almost equally on both factors with -.547 on Factor 1 and .532 on Factor 2. Consequently, this item did not demonstrate any meaningful interpretative value and therefore was not retained. Also, the visual display of the factor structure after rotation showed item 5 far isolated from the rest of the items as seen in the loading plot in Figure 15 (Appendix I). The implication of this item isolation in the loading plot is that item 5 may be assessing another construct other than the two emerging factors (Costello & Osborne, 2005). Since the GSBDS is a newly created scale, the exclusion of such a spurious item among host of others at the initial stages of instrument construction is explicable. Because it is detected now as not belonging to the scale, it was deleted from the group of items.

After deleting item 5, Cronbach's alpha for the GSBDS increased from .828 to .868. In addition, the cumulative percentage for the two factors increased from 61% to 64%. Factor 1 has communality values ranging from .666 to .821 while Factor 2 shows values ranging from .647 to .812. These results, as shown in Table 14, revealed that two orthogonal factors emerged as separate domains underlying the social distance construct. As a result of this finding, the two factors will be treated as two dependent variables in subsequent analyses of the study.

Table 14. *Factor Loadings for Principal Component Analysis with Varimax Rotation of the GSBDS*

Items	Factor 1	Factor 2
Admire her ideas	**.821**	-.233
Comfortable taking her orders	**.820**	.049
Admire her character	**.772**	.257
Vote her into a political office	.345	**.647**
Dropped for cross-loading	**-.547***	**.532***
Accept as an intimate friend	.085	**.812**
Support her promotion	**.724**	.338
Confide my secretes in her	.158	**.783**
Not defend her rights if they were Jeopardized	**.747**	.102
Have her as my mentor	**.666**	**.452**

Note. Factor loadings > .40 are in boldface. *Item 5 was dropped from the sub-scales for cross-loading.

Final Scales

Accommodative disposition domain. Factor 1 was labeled the *accommodative disposition domain* and comprised of six items. Reliability alpha for this subscale was .88 (Cronbach's α). As seen in Table 14, the items loading on this factor contain words with semantic imports conveying feelings of personal trust in and acceptance of one's stimulus person. To admire a person's ideas, to feel comfortable taking his/her orders, to admire his/her character, to defend his/her rights, to support his/her promotion, and to accept him/her as one's mentor all together reveal a sense of trust, likeness, support, and the willingness to accept the authority and opinion of such a stimulus person. With high communality values, the descriptor variables on this factor strongly show the willingness to accommodate the stimulus person under the various circumstances expressed in the items, hence, the name, accommodative disposition domain.

The one common denominator strongly underlying the import of all the six items on Factor 1 is the element of *trust* in the stimulus person's authority and ability. Item 10 cross-loaded onto Factor 2 but had a higher loading of .666 on Factor 1. Item 10 was therefore included on Factor 1 because it expresses the feeling of trust as represented in the items on Factor 1 more than it does the sense of invitation for relationship as expressed by items on Factor 2. This judgment of the researcher is based on the subjective assessment that the idea of accepting a person as a mentor more epitomizes the feeling of trust in that person than it does the invitation for relationship. The latter (invitation for relationship) as expressed by Factor 2, fits more with the *interpersonal affective disposition domain* - the name given to Factor 2 - and will be discussed in the next paragraph. Consequently, item 10 loaded on Factor 1 and will not be judged as cross-loading in this analysis.

Interpersonal affective disposition domain. The second scale was labeled *interpersonal affective disposition domain* and consists of three items with Cronbach's alpha reliability 0f .68. As seen in Table 14, the items loaded highly with communality values ranging from .647 to .812. In the Ghanaian socio-cultural milieu, to accept a person as one's intimate (close) friend suggests, among other things, the willingness to confide one's secrets in that person. (Note: Intimate friend in Ghanaian parlance simply means *close friend.*) Confiding one's secrets in a friend suggests the presence of trust being reposed in that consociate. Item 4, which expresses the willingness/ non-willingness to "vote her into a political office," may appear, at face value, to have loaded inappropriately on this factor. Furthermore, these three items forming *interpersonal affective disposition domain,* subjectively also indicate a propensity for a relational disposition. These items suggest invitation for relationship or friendship without strict boundaries.

It is important to note that politics and voting in Ghana are most often heavily expressive of ethnic feelings and affiliations. People vote for who they consider to be in their camp. Somebody they feel will relate with them and vouch for them without hesitation; someone they feel they know and who also knows them; someone they feel they can have interpersonal relationship with. Consequently, social ties and affiliations play a strong role in who gets voted into a political office in Ghana. Hence, expressing the willingness to vote a person into a political office then could be expressive of some underlying social affinity as the motivating factor. With that at the backdrop, it makes sense then to include item 4 (*I would/ would not vote her into a political office*) as a meaningful descriptor sharing the variance with items 8 and 6 in explaining the interpersonal affective disposition domain. Collectively, therefore, the items on the *interpersonal affective disposition domain,* which demonstrate affection and epitomize the willingness to relate with one's stimulus person with negligible or no social distance.

This coefficient shows a moderate internal consistency reliability of the subscale. It is accepted based on the following reason: one, since this is an exploratory study it is acceptable for Cronbach's alpha to yield 0.60 or greater (Simon, 2008). Second, the summated scale has only three items. This could explain why the alpha reliability reduced; there is the likelihood of the alpha value increasing with additional items on the scale, which future revisions of the scale could take note of. However, with Cronbach's alpha of .868 for the GSBDS prior to the creation of the two subscales, the robustness of scale reliability is established. This reliability coefficient of the GSBDS (.868) gives me the confidence to accept the subjective value of .682 for its subscale (*interpersonal affective disposition domain*) as a moderately reliable measure to be used in this study.

In summary, the PCA revealed that two factors emerged and were labeled the "accommodative disposition domain" and "interpersonal affective disposition domain." The interpersonal affective disposition domain sub-scale has only a moderate Cronbach's alpha (α = .68), which is lower than the conventional alpha of .80. However, this sub-scale was accepted based on the recommendation of Simon (2008) that an alpha reliability point of .60 may be accepted in an exploratory study. Consequently, the sub-scale will be cautiously used with the accommodative disposition domain sub-scale as the two criterion variables of the study.

Testing of Assumptions Results

Ratio of Cases to Independent Variables

Two appropriate determinations were made to match the ratio of cases to independent variables of the study: one for the multiple regression and the other for the individual predictors of the study. The formula for multiple correlation was computed: $N \geq 50 + 8m$ whereby m is the number of predictors in the model. For testing individual predictors, the formula $N \geq 104 + m$ was used. According to Tabachnick and Fidell (2001), the assumption here is that this will provide for the medium-size relationship between the independent variables and the dependent variable. For this study, testing for the multiple correlation required the calculation of the following: $N \geq 50 + 8 \times 4$, which yielded $N \geq 82$. Testing for individual independent variables ($N \geq 104 + 4$; $N \geq 108$), yielded $N \geq 108$ (314 ≥ 108). Thus, the sample size (N = 314) in this study exceeded these criteria, thereby meeting the assumption. Also, with 314 valid cases for N and 4 independent variables a ratio of 78.5 to 1 satisfied the minimum requirement of 5 to 1 cases as required.

Multicollinearity

The Variance Inflation Factor (VIF) for the independent variables revealed that no statistically significant multicollinearity existed among the independent variables included in the model, $p > .001$ (see Tables K1 and K2 in Appendix K). All of the independent variables yielded a VIF below the criterion of 5.0 and thus no significant multicollinearity was observed.

Normality and Multivariate Outliers

A Mahalanobis Distance (MD) was conducted for all four independent variables. The MD was evaluated with $p < .001$ and degrees of freedom 4. A Chi-square score of 15.010 was obtained, which falls below the Chi-Square test critical value of 18.47 indicating no statistically significant multivariate outliers (see Table L1 in Appendix L). A visual inspection of the scatterplot matrices (Q-Q plots) was further conducted of the continuous variables of the study (age, degree of egalitarianism, accommodative disposition, and interpersonal affective disposition). Indications for bivariate and potential multivariate outliers were observed in the variable distributions (see Figures L1 – L13 in Appendix L). Z-standardized scores were computed for these continuous level variables to confirm the existence of significant univariate outliers. All variables were within the acceptable range of -3.0 to +3.0 (required for sample sizes over 80). According to Stevens (1996), if $N > 100$, then outliers are $Z > +/- 4.0$. The age standardized variable revealed one score above +/-3 (3.42) indicating the presence of an outlier.

Furthermore, skewness and kurtosis test was also computed using SPSS frequency distribution command. Age and accommodative disposition variables again showed slight indications of positive skewness. With a standard error of skewness at .138, age has a skewness of .425, kurtosis of -.498 and accommodative disposition has a skewness of .531 and kurtosis of -.678.

Also, a Shapiro-Wilk test was conducted to test for multivariate normality of the continuous variables across the groups. As shown in Table L2 (in Appendix L), the test was significant for age and accommodative disposition variables by gender and lineage tie. Age was significant by gender for both male and female ($p < .001$) with degrees of freedom 174 and 140 respectively. With the same degrees of freedom for all relationships by gender, degree of egalitarianism was not significant by gender for male ($p > .05$) but was significant by female ($p < .05$). Accommodative disposition was significant by both male and female (p < .001) and interpersonal affective disposition was significant by both genders (p < .01). Degree of egalitarianism was not significant by male (p > .05) but was significant for female (p < .05).

By lineage tie, age, accommodative disposition, and interpersonal affective disposition of the respondents showed skewness violating multivariate normality (see Tables L2 in Appendix L). Age by lineage tie was significant for both patrilineal (p < .01) and matrilineal (p < .001) with degrees of freedom 166 and 148 respectfully. With the same degrees of freedom, accommodative disposition was again significant by lineage tie (p < .001). Interpersonal affective disposition was also significant by patrilineal tie (p < .01) and matrilineal tie (p < .01). Degree of egalitarianism was not significant by patrilineal tie (p > .05) but was significant by matrilineal tie (p < .05). Consequently, a determination was made to transform these continuous level variables prior to the regression analyses. The results of data distribution for all variables after the transformation are presented in Appendix M. The histograms demonstrate normal distribution of scores with normal curves for all study variables, thus addressing prior data anomalies (see Figure M1 – M6).

Linearity and Homoscedasticity

The results of the tests conducted earlier for the MR assumptions showed that assumptions for linearity and homoscedasticity are, by presumption, also met (Tabachnick & Fidell, 2001). However, scatterplots of the predicted values of the dependent variables ($\hat{Y}$) against residuals were conducted. An examination of the scatterplots in Appendix M yielded conclusive results (see Figures M7, M8, M9, M10). The scatterplots generated showed nearly oblong or rectangular shapes indicating linearity of relationship (though weak) between predicted variables scores and errors of prediction. The residuals have a linear relationship with the criterion variables (accommodative disposition and interpersonal affective disposition variables). These transformed variables were used for analysis in this study instead of their raw scores.

Multiple Regressions

A simultaneous multiple regression (SMR) was conducted to test whether lineage tie, gender, age, and degree of egalitarianism share significant relationships with teachers' self-reported degree of accommodative disposition and interpersonal affective disposition (social distance). This data analytic strategy allowed for the retention of the continuous nature of the variables and also made it possible to examine the independent effects of each predictor variable. The analytic strategy also allowed for the examination of the interactive effect of predictors found being significant contributors. To do this latter analysis, the main effect terms for predictors found to have significant association with the predicted variable(s) were all standardized. Predicted values ($\hat{Y}s$) were computed for representative high and low groups 1 standard deviation above and below the mean, setting the alpha level at .05 (see Appendix N.1).

Two sets of regression analyses were then run to test variables association within the conceptual framework of the research hypotheses. The first model tested predictor variables' association with the interpersonal affective disposition domain. The second model examined predictors' association with the accommodative disposition domain. The scores for the predictors found with significant association were standardized to compare their unique effects as mentioned above. A third regression therefore was run to examine these effects (see Table 17).

Predicting Interpersonal Affective Disposition Domain

Correlational analyses were conducted to test the association between interpersonal affective disposition and the predictor variables of lineage tie, gender, age, and degree of egalitarianism. Table N2 (see Appendix N) presents the two-tailed Pearson correlation matrix of variables' associations. As shown in Table N2, there was no significant association between the predictors and the interpersonal affective disposition of teachers. Lineage tie was not significantly associated with teachers' interpersonal affective disposition ($r = .031$, $p > .05$). Teachers' gender did not show statistical significant association with their interpersonal disposition either ($r = .064$, $p > .05$). Age of teachers also showed no statistical significant association with teachers' interpersonal affective disposition ($r = -.060$, $p > .05$). The degree of egalitarianism of teachers also showed no statistical significance association with the interpersonal affective disposition of teachers ($r = .015$, $p > .05$). However, there was statistically significant but weak association between teachers' age and their degree of egalitarianism ($r = .171$, $p < .01$). This positive correlation indicates a corresponding increase in scores between the two variables, implying that teachers, who reported higher scores on the age index, also reported having greater degree of egalitarianism. Or conversely, as teachers' age decrease, their scores on degree of egalitarianism also decrease. Thus, the older the teacher, the more egalitarian he or she is and the younger the teacher, the lesser his or her degree of egalitarianism.

The overall result of the multiple regression for interpersonal affective disposition was not statistically significant, $R^2 = .006$, $R^2_{adj} = -.006$, $F(4, 309) = .504$, $p > .05$. The R squared value indicated that the combined effect of this model only accounted for .06% of the variance in the predicted variable (interpersonal affective disposition). Thus, with a p value of .733, this model did not demonstrate any association between the four predictors and the predicted; the combined effect of lineage tie, age, gender, and degree of egalitarianism did not significantly predict interpersonal affective disposition of teachers. A summary of the regression coefficients for this model is presented in Table 15 indicating that none of the four predictors significantly contributed to the model. Figure 3 gives a visual representation of the contribution of each predictor in the model.

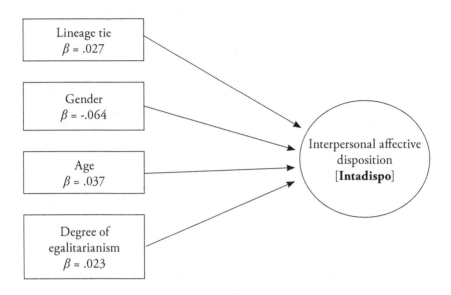

Figure 3. *Weight of prediction of interpersonal affective disposition by the four predictors*

Predicting the Accommodative Disposition Domain

Correlation analyses were conducted to examine the association between accommodative disposition and the four predictors: lineage tie, gender, age, and degree of egalitarianism.

Table N3 (see Appendix N) presents a Pearson correlation matrix of the individual associations of the predictor variables with the accommodative disposition

Table 15. *Simultaneous Multiple Regression Analysis Summary for Lineage Ties, Age, Gender, and Egalitarianism Predicting Interpersonal Affective Disposition Domain of Social Distance (N = 314)*

Model	Unstandardized		Standardized			Correlations	
	B	SE	β	t	p	Zero-order	Partial r
Lineage Ties	.072	.149	.027	.483	.629	.031	.027
Gender	.098	.150	.037	.650	.516	.039	.037
Age1	-.678	.607	-.064	-1.117	.265	-.060	-.063
Egalitarianism1	.001	.002	.023	.393	.695	.015	.022

Note. $R^2 = .006$; $R^2_{adjusted} = -.006$; $F(4,309) = .504$, $p > .05$. ¹Transformed variable. subscale.

The results revealed that only age and degree of egalitarianism made small to medium effects, respectively, in their unique contributions in explaining the percentage of variance in accommodative disposition. The observed associations were negative and only one of them (degree of egalitarianism with accommodative disposition), was in the expected direction. These inverse associations of the two significant predictors with accommodative disposition indicate that higher scores on age and degree of egalitarianism variables are expected to have lower scores on the accommodative disposition subscale of the social distance scale. By implication, teachers who reported higher scores on these two significant predictors revealed lesser scores on social distance. Thus, older teachers were seen to have lesser social distance (expressed in accommodative disposition) towards their headmistress ($r = -.202$, $p < .001$). So, age explains about 20% of the variance in accommodative disposition. Subsequently, teachers who reported being more egalitarian also showed they have lesser social distance (expressed in accommodative disposition), towards their headmistress ($r = -.299$, $p < .001$). Thus, degree of egalitarianism explains about 30% of the variance in teachers' accommodative disposition.

As can be observed in Table N3 (Appendix N), there were no significant association of gender and lineage tie of teachers with the accommodative disposition subscale. Gender was not significant ($r = .023$, $p > .05$), indicating that teachers' gender (whether male or female), showed no meaningful association with teachers' social distance (expressed in accommodative disposition) of the sample studied. Likewise, lineage tie of teachers (whether matrilineal or patrilineal) did not show any importance association with teachers' perceived social distance ($r = .066$, $p > .05$).

A simultaneous multiple regression was conducted to assess the individual contribution of the predictors. The results indicated that this model was statistically significant, $R^2 = .120$, $R^2_{adjusted} = .108$, $F(4,309) = 10.511$, $p < .001$. The overall effect of the four predictors significantly accounted for 12% of the variance in teachers' accommodative disposition, which according to Cohen (1988), is about medium size effect. Table 15 presents the summary of the regression coefficients of the unique contribution of each individual predictor. Of the predictors investigated, both age ($\beta = -.155$, $p < .01$) and degree of egalitarianism ($\beta = -.277$, $p < .001$) were statistically significant predictors of teachers' perceived accommodative disposition. Lineage tie ($\beta = .067$, $p > .05$) and gender ($\beta = .041$, $p > .05$) showed no statistical significance in predicting accommodative disposition. The matrix also shows which variable made the strongest contribution in predicting social distance of teachers (expressed in accommodative disposition) to wards headmistresses.

As can be seen in Table 16, degree of egalitarianism and age had significance but with negative regression weights (standardized coefficients beta), after each controlling for the other variables in the model. The effect size measures indicating the practical or clinical significance of the predictions are also shown in Table 16. After controlling for or partialing out the effects of other variables the partial effect size for degree of egalitarianism was $r = -.279$ ($t = -5.107$, $p < .001$). This means, for instance, that after accounting for age, lineage tie, and gender, teachers with greater perceived degree of egalitarianism accounted for 28% of the variance in teachers' accommodative disposition measure. This, according to Cohen (1988), is a fairly medium effect size. Likewise for age, younger teachers have greater scores on accommodative disposition (social distance), showing a partial effect size of $r = -.161$ (t -2.86, $p < .01$). Thus, age, after controlling for all other variables, accounted for 16% of the meaning in teachers' accommodative disposition. As can be seen in Table 16, the standardized beta values of the regression matrix indicated that degree of egalitarianism was the strongest predictor of accommodative disposition (β = -.28, t = -5.11, p < .05), followed by age (β = -.16, t = -2.86, p < .05). Lineage tie (β = .07, t = 1.26, p > .05), and gender (β = .04, t = .76, p > .05) were not significant predictors.

Table 16. *Simultaneous Multiple Regression Analysis Summary for Lineage Ties, Age, Gender, and Egalitarianism Predicting Accommodative Disposition Domain of Social Distance (N = 314)*

Model	Unstandardized		Standardized			Correlations	
	B	SE	β	t	p	Zero-order	Partial r
Lineage Ties	.025	.020	.067	1.257	.210	.066	.071
Gender	.015	.020	.041	.764	.445	.023	.043
Age[1]	-.232	.081	-.155**	-2.860	.005	.202	.161
Egalitarianism[1]	-.001	.000	-.277***	-5.107	.000	-.299	-.279

Note. R^2 = .120; $R^2_{adjusted}$ = .108; $F(4,309)$ = 10.511, ** = p < .01, *** = p < .001 .
[1]Transformed variable

Based on the findings that only age and degree of egalitarianism made significant contribution in predicting accommodative disposition, the effects of the significant contributors were compared to the effects in the full model. To do this, the non-significant predictors were removed from the model and another regression was run by entering only age and degree of egalitarianism in the regression analysis. Variables were entered using the Stepwise method, which combined both forward and backward procedures to address the possibility of an entering variable weakening the predictive value of the other (George & Mallery, 2011). The effects of the interaction between age and degree of egalitarianism were explored (Tabachnick & Fidell, 2001). Z-scores were created for age and degree of egalitarianism to remove unit of measurement from the coefficients so as to compare the standardized *Beta* coefficients in interpreting the relative importance of each predictor (Tabachnick & Fidell, 2001). The interactive influence of the two predictors (age and degree of egalitarianism) was compared with their substantive effects in the full model.

Table 17 showed results of the analysis indicating no improvement in the substantive β values for the age and egalitarianism variables. The interactive effect was significant with $R^2 = .113$; $F(2, 311) = 19.85$, $p < .001$. Again, the *age* variable accounted for 16% of variance on the *accommodative disposition* variable while egalitarianism accounted for 27% of variance on the *accommodative disposition* variable (an increase of .4%). Thus, no significant differences were observed between the standardized scores and the effect of the raw scores (age and egalitarianism).

The interactive effect of *age* and *egalitarianism* on accommodative disposition produced an R^2 *of* .113, indicating that 11.3% of variance in the predicted was accounted for by the interactive effect of the two predictors appreciating only .7% increase in variance accounted for in accommodative disposition compared to their contribution in the full model. The practical significance for age and degree of egalitarianism of teachers demonstrated small to medium effect sizes. Partial effect size for age was $r = -.161$ ($t = -2.874$, $p < .01$) and partial effect size for degree of egalitarianism was $r = -.274$ ($t = -5.034$, $p < .001$). Thus, age accounted for 16% of the variance in accommodative disposition while degree of egalitarianism accounted for 27% of that variance. Again, this percentage is consistent with the percentage of the combined effect of all four predictors on accommodative disposition of teachers.

Table 17. *Regression Coefficients of Standardized Scores for Degree of Egalitarianism and Age of Respondents Showing the Interactive Effect of the Two Predictors on Accommodative Disposition*

Model	Unstandardized		Standardized			Correlations	
	B	SE	β	t	p	Zero- order	Partial r (R^2)
'Accodispo	1.196	.010	-	120.498	.000		
tzAge	-.029	.010	-.156	-2.874**	.004	-.202	-.161
tzEgalitarianism	-.051	.010	-.273	-5.034***	.000	-.299	-.274
Age by Egalitarianism							(R^2) .113

Note: Accodispo = Accommodative Disposition Domain (Criterion variable). $R^2 = .113$; R^2 adjusted = .108; $F(2, 311) = 19.855$, * $= p < .05$, ** $= p < .01$, *** $= p < .001$; ' = transformed variable; z = standardized predictors with z-scores

CHAPTER V

SUMMARY, CONCLUSIONS AND IMPLICATIONS

Introduction

This chapter comprises of three major sections. The first section gives a concise summary of the theoretical framework undergirding the study and the procedure used for the analyses. The second section discusses the research results vis-à-vis the literature reviewed and a conclusion. The third section consists of study implications, the limitations of the study and recommendation for scholars and stakeholders of school administration. This study was an exploratory research investigating the association between teachers' lineage ties, teachers' age, teachers' gender, and their degree of egalitarianism (as predictors) and teachers' social distance towards their headmistresses.

Scholars that investigated discrimination against women concluded that social distance is symptomatic of a male-*hegemonious* culture. Such cultures perceive the female group as subordinates to men, especially during decision making. There is consensus among these scholars that such subservient views of women are products of the socio-cultural orientation generally shared by both men and women (Aird, n.d; Ameh, 2002; Amoakohene, 2004; Awumbila, 2001; Ben-Ari, 2001; Lobel, Mashraki-Pedhatzur, Mantzur, & Libby, 2000). Like all other women bosses, female heads of second cycle schools in Ghana also suffer the pang of the gender discrimination and its associated negative attitudes from their subordinates (Oduro & Macbeath, 2003). Some of the cross-cultural studies that investigated discrimination against women administrators also established links between demographic variables and social distance towards these female heads as central to their investigations (Shapira, Arar, & Azaiza, 2010; Skrla, Reyes, & Scheurich, 2000; Triandis & Davis, 1965). However, no such studies in Ghana have been noted in the literature as specifically investigating variables such as lineage ties, gender, age and degree of egalitarianism as the correlates of social distance towards female heads of schools.

I did an eclectic review of literature revealing evidences of discriminatory attitude towards female heads of schools, cross-culturally, and then narrowing it specifically on paradigms among second cycle institutions in Ghana. A link was drawn between gender ideological beliefs that view female as inferior to men and evidences of non-cooperative behavior on the part of subordinates towards female principals (typically called in Ghana as headmistresses). This current study attempts an exploration of how such views (as seen in other cultures), impacted the degree of interpersonal relationship (defined in this study as social distance) between teachers and their headmistresses in Ghana.

The literature showed that some investigation was done in Ghana on discrimination against women domestically and at workplaces and also on teachers' negative attitudes towards headmistresses as a result of gender stereotypical views of them (Gedzi, 2009; Oduro & Macbeath, 2003; Sossou, 2006; Tsikata, 1997). However, not much is seen on how those views affected teachers' social distance with their headmistresses. What is specifically missing in those few qualitative studies on Ghana, is the lack of investigation of the socio-demographic-ideological variables such as lineage ties, age, gender, and the degree of egalitarianism as probable correlates of social distance between teachers and headmistresses. The need to explore the association of these variables is the central focus of this study.

Review of the Theoretical Framework

Even though the study was not a test of theories, two theoretical perspectives were employed to explain the conceptual *raison d'être* undergirding the exploration of teachers' perceived degree of egalitarianism and its effect on teachers' social distance with headmistresses. Symbolic interactionism and embedded group theory offer this conceptual framework. As discussed earlier, symbolic interactionism postulates that people's attitude towards objects is determined by the kind of views or perceptions they have of that objects (Lynch & McConatha, 2006; Rosenbaum, 2009). Embedded group theory suggests that historical perspectives are important in understanding groups or organizational identity and behavior (Alderfer & Smith, 1982). In other words, human beings have multiple identities and behavioral patterns that must be understood within the framework of their corporate culture. Such a shared culture, for instance, may explain why teachers of second cycle institutions within the Ghanaian male hegemonious culture will relate negatively towards the authority of a headmistress.

Specifically, as supported by research hypotheses 1, 2, and 5, these theoretical frameworks could lend explanation to why teachers, degree of egalitarianism, *par excellence,* and age were important in explaining teachers' degree of social distance with their headmistress.

As found in this current study, teachers who are more egalitarian in the expression of their gender ideological belief reported having less social distance with their headmistresses. This means that the less egalitarian teachers are, the greater or wider their social distance will be toward a headmistress. In other words, teachers with traditional gender ideological views (expressing male hegemony and female subordination) will have greater social distance with their headmistress. These findings reverberate the findings of Oduro and MacBeath (2003), who revealed that some older male teachers in some Ghanaian schools of their study resented the authority of their headmistress simply because she was a woman. In fact, these researchers reported that one of the female heads was reminded, during a staff meeting, she should not forget that she is a female, a subordinate and was yelled at to drop her views and accept the decisions of her male (subordinate) teachers.

Thus, while symbolic interactionism attempts an explanation of why teachers resent female authority of their school heads, embedded group theory gives such resentment a corporate character. This means that the type of perception teachers have of their headmistresses is not just an isolated, individual idiosyncratic behavior but rather a group behavior, embodied in the societal expressions of cultural norms generally shared by both men and women (Briles, 1999).

Statement of Study Procedure

The data for this study came from 12 selected second cycle institutions from the two main lineage blocs (patrilineal and matrilineal blocs) in Ghana; six from each lineage bloc. Through a combination of purposive and snowball sampling approach, a multi-level non-randomized sampling rounded off 314 teachers for this study. Because of the absence of previous research specifically investigating the problem of the study as mentioned above, an exploratory research design was deemed appropriate for the analysis of the study data. Two valid and reliable instruments (SRES and GSBDS) were administered to teachers to measure degree of egalitarianism and social distance respectively.

A factor analysis (PCA) of the GSBDS revealed two orthogonal factors resulting into the creation of two sub-scales (accommodative disposition scale and interpersonal affective disposition scale) for GSBDS. These subscales were treated as the two dependent variables of the study. This dichotomy has made a departure from the unidimensionality of the social distance construct to bi-dimensional, distinct subscales of the social distance construct. Hypotheses were derived from the theoretical framework of the literature reviewed and were examined using simultaneous multiple regression (SMR) analysis.

Testing the Results with the Research Hypotheses

Model 1

Hypothesis 1. It was hypothesized that the degree of egalitarianism, lineage tie, gender, and age of teachers, in second cycle institutions in

Ghana significantly relate to and predict teachers' perceived interpersonal affective disposition toward their headmistress. The results of this estimated model showed that the predictors did not significantly predict teachers' interpersonal affective disposition towards headmistresses of their schools. The null hypothesis was not rejected at the .05 level ($F = .504$; $p = .733$). Thus, lineage tie, gender, age and degree of egalitarianism of teachers showed no significant contribution in explaining the variance in teachers' interpersonal affective disposition.

Hypothesis 2. It was hypothesized that the higher the degree of egalitarianism reported by the teachers, the lesser their scores in perceived interpersonal affective disposition towards their headmistress. Results from the analysis revealed that no significant association was found between teachers' degree of egalitarianism and their interpersonal affective disposition at the .05 alpha level ($\beta = .023$, $p = .695$). Thus, the test failed to reject the null hypothesis. Consequently, this research finding does not support the research hypothesis that the higher teachers' degree of egalitarianism the lesser their scores in interpersonal affective disposition with their headmistress. Evidently only 2.3% of variance was accounted for by this effect on teachers' perceived interpersonal affective disposition towards headmistresses (see Table 15).

Hypothesis 3. It was hypothesized that teachers of matrilineal descent will have lesser scores on perceived interpersonal affective disposition (lesser social distance) towards their headmistress than their patrilineal counterparts. Again, this research hypothesis was not supported by the study results. The null hypothesis was not rejected at .05 ($\beta = .027$, $p = .629$). As a result, lineage tie did not show any significant difference between matrilineal and patrilineal in prediction teachers' interpersonal affective disposition nor was lineage, per se, significantly associated with teachers' interpersonal affective disposition. As can be seen in Table 15, the standardized beta value shows that only 3% of variance was accounted for by this predictor in explaining teachers' interpersonal affective disposition.

Hypothesis 4. It was hypothesized that the female teachers will have lesser scores on perceived interpersonal affective disposition towards their headmistress than the male teachers. Contrary to expectations, this research hypothesis was not supported by the study findings. The null hypothesis failed to be rejected at the .05 alpha level (β = .037, p = .516). Gender of teachers, therefore, did not show any significant association (4% of variance explained) with teachers' interpersonal affective disposition. Evidently, gender differential was irrelevant in the absence of any significant association between the predictor and the predicted. Therefore, the hypothesis that female teachers rather than their male counterparts will have lesser scores on perceived interpersonal affective disposition toward their headmistress was not supported.

Hypothesis 5. It was hypothesized that the younger the teachers, the lesser their scores on perceived interpersonal affective disposition (lesser social distance) towards their headmistress. Results from the analysis revealed that there is no significant association between age and teachers' perceived interpersonal affective disposition toward their headmistress. As a result, age differential could not be determined in explaining teachers' perceived interpersonal affective disposition. The null hypothesis, therefore, could not be rejected at .05 alpha level ((β = -.064, p = .265). Only 6.4% of the variance in perceived interpersonal affective disposition was accounted for by teachers' age (see Table 15).

Hypothesis 6. It was hypothesized that degree of egalitarianism of teachers in second cycle institutions in Ghana will be the strongest predictor of teachers' perceived interpersonal affective disposition toward their headmistress. This research hypothesis was also not supported since the overall model was not statistically significant and the unique effect of degree of egalitarianism was not statistically significant either. Thus, the null hypothesis failed to be rejected at .05 alpha level (F = .504; p = .733) for the overall model and (β = .023, p = .695) for degree of egalitarianism.

Model 2

Hypothesis 1. It was hypothesized that the degree of egalitarianism, lineage ties, gender, and age of teachers, in second cycle institutions in Ghana significantly relate to and predict teachers' accommodative disposition towards their headmistress. The results of this estimated model demonstrated that the predictors systematically, significantly predicted teachers' accommodative disposition towards headmistresses of their schools. Even though the result of this estimated model showed that the null hypothesis was rejected at .05 level (F = 12.78; p = .000), only two of the predictors (age and degree of egalitarianism) showed any statistical significance at the .05 level (see Table 16). Thus, this research finding supports the hypothesis that the combined effect of degree of egalitarianism, lineage tie, gender and age did influence teachers' accommodative disposition (social distance). With this finding, the null hypothesis is rejected and the alternative hypothesis is accepted.

Hypothesis 2. It was hypothesized that the higher the degree of egalitarianism reported by teachers, the lesser their perceived social distance towards their headmistress. It is thus statistically significant at .05 alpha level (β = -.277, p = 000). The weight of the association suggested an inverse correlation with accommodative disposition. Consequently, this research finding supports the hypothesis that teachers with more egalitarian views reported lesser social distance (accommodative disposition) with their headmistresses. The null hypothesis then is rejected and the alternative hypothesis accepted. With this significant relationship observed then, our prediction of younger teachers having more egalitarian views with the consequential lesser social distance with headmistresses was not support. Rather, older-age (older teachers) were found to be more egalitarian and have closer social distance with their headmistresses.

Hypothesis 3. It was hypothesized that teachers of matrilineal descent will have lesser perceived social distance towards their headmistress than their patrilineal counterparts. Results from the analysis revealed that no significant association was found between lineage tie and teachers' accommodative disposition at .05 alpha level (β = .067, p = .210). Thus, the test failed to reject the null hypothesis. Consequently, this research finding does not support the research hypothesis that teachers of matrilineal descent will show lesser social distance with their headmistress than will their patrilineal counterparts. Evidently, lineage tie does not seem to have any significant influence (about 7% effect) on teachers' perceived social distance towards headmistresses (see Table 16).

Hypothesis 4. It was hypothesized that female teachers will have lesser-perceived social distance towards their headmistress than the male teachers. However, this hypothesis was not supported by the research finding. Gender did not show any significant association with teachers' accommodative disposition variable at the .05 alpha level (β = .041, p = .445); the null hypothesis could, therefore, not be rejected. That teachers' gender failed to show any significant systematic influence in predicting teachers' accommodative disposition towards their headmistresses, makes gender a non-influential variable in this study. For this study, this means that whether teachers were male or female was not important in the prediction of their social distance towards their headmistresses.

Hypothesis 5. It was hypothesized that the younger the teachers, the lesser their social distance towards their headmistress. As presented in Table 16, this hypothetical assumption was not supported by the research finding even though there was a significant relationship. The result of the model showed significant association between teachers' age and their accommodative disposition at .05 alpha level (β = -.155, p = 005) but the negative β value for this relationship indicates an inverse correlation in the direction of association. By implication, a decrease in age will associate with an increase in perceived social distance. Consequently, the younger teachers are, the greater their social distance (expressed in accommodative disposition), towards headmistresses. This finding is contrary to the research expectation. Older teachers are therefore shown to be better disposed toward interpersonal relationship with their headmistress than younger teachers are. The null hypothesis for this model, therefore, failed to be rejected.

Hypothesis 6. It was hypothesized that degree of egalitarianism of teachers in second cycle institutions in Ghana will be the strongest predictor of teachers' perceived social distance toward a headmistress. The *ANOVA* test was statistically significant $F(4, 309)$ = 10.511, p = .000, supporting the hypothesis. Table 16 shows the β values for all predictions. The β weight for degree of egalitarianism was 28%, followed by age (16%). Lineage tie and gender followed with 7% and 4%, respectively. Thus, the degree of teachers' egalitarianism emerged as the strongest predictor among the four predictors in determining teachers' social distance (accommodative disposition) towards their headmistresses. The null hypothesis is, therefore, rejected and the alternative hypothesis accepted.

Summary

The primary concern of this study is to test the utility of the four predictor variables namely lineage ties, age, gender, and the degree of egalitarianism of teachers from second cycle institutions in Ghana in predicting teachers' social distance towards their headmistresses. However, the result of a factor analysis of the criterion variable (social distance) revealed two distinct subscales from the factor loadings of the Eigen values. These substantive subscales were treated as two orthogonal criterion variables named according to the functional definition of their lexes. Thus the social distance construct generated two domains namely, the accommodative disposition domain and the interpersonal affective domain variables as the criterion variables of this study.

Evidence from the simultaneous multiple regression analyses revealed that no interactions were significant for the four predictors when regressed on the interpersonal affective disposition variable. However, of the four predictors, only the degree of egalitarianism and the age of teachers from second cycle institutions in Ghana demonstrated any significant impact in determining teachers' social distance towards their headmistresses when regressed on the accommodative disposition variable. That the prediction of social distance was only relevant for the accommodative disposition domain of the construct and, not at all for the interpersonal affective disposition variable, calls for a reexamination of the latter variable *vis a vis* its utility as a domain of the social distance construct. This limitation will be discussed later in this chapter.

Comparing Research Findings with the Literature

In this section, comparison of research findings with the literature was done. The association of each independent variable with social distance was discussed within the theoretical context of the current literature. Directly, the results of the association between lineage ties and social distance were compared with established links in the literature reviewed. Similar comparisons were done of gender, age, and degree of egalitarianism with evidence from the literature. Six specific research hypotheses were derived from two major research questions and were tested against the backdrop of current literature. The major research questions are:

1. Do the degree of egalitarianism, lineage ties, sex, and age of teachers in second cycle institutions in Ghana statistically and practically significantly relate to and predict their perceived social distance towards their headmistress?

2. Are there any differentials in the degree of egalitarianism, lineage affiliation, gender, and age of teachers in second cycle institutions of Ghana in predicting their social distance with a headmistress? If so, which variable is the strongest predictor of teachers' social distance with their headmistress in second cycle institutions in Ghana: degree of egalitarianism, lineage affiliation, gender, or age?

Lineage Tie and Teachers' Social Distance

Lineage tie, which is matrilineal or patrilineal descent of teachers, is postulated to predict social distance (interpersonal relationship) of teachers in second cycle institutions of Ghana with their headmistresses. Current literature on Ghana has established no direct link between lineage tie and the social distance construct. Assumptions made of this association were based on some emphases made of the role lineage ties play in ascribing statuses to societal members within the Ghanaian culture. And yet, the literature on the role of lineage tie, per se, in Ghana is scanty and related solely to inheritance and decision-making privileges of societal members (Gedzi, 2009; Takyi & Gyimah, 2007). Ghana is one of the few cultures of sub-Saharan Africa with duo-lineage descent. While people of the patrilineal descent trace inheritance prerogatives along their fathers' line, progenies of matrilineal descent trace theirs along their mothers' line (Kannae, 1993; Takyi & Broughton, 2006; Takyi & Gyimah, 2007). These scholars have advanced the argument that, since inheritance and property acquisition privileges make individuals prominent in the Ghanaian society, one's lineage tie and gender within a given lineage bloc shape and define one's authority and status within that given lineage system. Hence, the assumption was made that even though Ghana is generally patriarchal, women from the matrilineal system may enjoy better leverage than women from the patrilineal system with regard to decision-making privileges, *par excellence.*

Nukunya (1987) for instance concluded that the status ascribed to lineage members do shape and emphasize society's perception of and attitude towards these lineage members. Conceptually, then, society's response towards such socio-cultural arrangements will favor a more appreciation for the authority of a female head in a matrilineal system than will be favored of her in a patrilineal system. In other words, teachers from the matrilineal system are presumed to be more appreciative of a female authority and thus become more favorable towards having an interpersonal relationship with their headmistress than will the teachers from the patrilineal system. Hypothetically, then, teachers of matrilineal descent were expected to have lesser social distance with their headmistress than their patrilineal counterparts. Contrary to this expectation, however, the third hypothesis was not supported by the research findings. Lineage tie did not show any statistically significant effect in predicting social distance of teachers towards headmistresses.

It is important to note that, nowhere in the literature has the direct effect of lineage tie been linked to perceived social distance. It is possible that the indirect inferences made to proposition this expected association between lineage tie and social distance may have been weakened by other observations made earlier by Kannae (1993) and Takyi and Broughton (2006). These researchers, in respect of the pervasiveness of patriarchy in Ghana, have warned that even in matrilineal societies male supremacy has never been compromised; and that women may lose their place to men when it comes to leadership and authority prerogatives. Other factors such as the Interstate Succession Act, 1985 (PNDCL 111), which bequeaths the property of deceased husbands (who died without a will), to their wives and children instead of to their sisters' children in matrilineal societies, may have gradually eroded the influence of *matrilinealism* from the Ghanaian socio-cultural thinking. If the non-significant result of this current study has anything to do with the above probable cause, then the argument can be made that kinship or lineage tie is losing its once-upon-a-time held influence.

Gender and Social Distance

It was projected in this study that female teachers will have lesser perceived social distance towards their headmistress than the male teachers. More than anything, this assumption appealed to the sympathy of women toward a fellow out-group member, whose earned position must be protected and preserved. It also makes sense that members of the out-group (women) should opt for egalitarian views than men, who see their rightful position in society as leaders. In other words, gender will play a role in determining how the teacher population perceives their headmistresses and to what extent they are willing to trade interpersonal relationship with them (headmistresses). The idea of gender differentials in predicting teachers' social distance, therefore, derived from the assumption that there is an inherent conflict between the sexes in legitimizing their right and authority in occupying positions of leadership. Thus, each gender group has a justification for the legitimacy of their occupancy of leadership roles.

In the literature reviewed, a strong argument made about perception and how that shapes human attitude towards oneself and towards one's stimulus person (Awumbila, 2001; Briles, 1999; Fagenson, 1993; Triandis, 1977). Triandis (1971), for instance discussed the development of perception and how that translates into action response. Triandis maintained that it is the understanding a person has of an object of perception and how that cognition informs and initiates a belief response that determines how a person acts and reacts towards his or her object of perception. Other arguments made in the literature include the proposition that patriarchal societies are unfamiliar with women ascending to leadership positions (Andes, 1992; Gazso, 2003; Giannopoulos, Conway & Mendelson, 2005: Rashotte & Webster, 2005) hence, any disenfranchisement of women from leadership roles is a natural reaction of society's unfamiliarity with this *new wave* of women becoming leaders. Others insisted that the norm of ascribing leadership roles solely to men is a vestige of cultural indoctrination and women need to emancipate themselves from such brainwashing (Ardayfio-Schandorf, 2005; Briles, 1999; Tanye, 2008). The consensus is that men were found to be less egalitarian than women, thus, favoring a traditionalist perspective of male supremacy over women

(Oduro & MacBEath, 2003). It is against this backdrop that I venture the proposition that it is potentially challenging for a male teacher with such traditionalist orientation to work under a female boss (the headmistress of his school).

The occupancy of headship position by the headmistress may therefore be seen as a breach of the cultural norm that reserves leadership roles for men. A person with such traditionally ingrained patriarchal feelings could resent the authority of the headmistress. This latter relationship was evident from the result of this study when degree of egalitarianism correlated with accommodative disposition (social distance of teachers). But where is the role of gender in the dynamics of this correlation?

The hypothesis that there will be gender differentials in teachers' perceived social distance with their female headmistresses did not show any significant relationship with the accommodative disposition measure. The results of the test of significance in this study did not support the fourth hypothesis that female teachers, more than their male counterparts, will have lesser social distance towards their headmistress. In fact, gender did not show any significant association with teachers' social distance. As seen in Table 16, only 4% of the variance in social distance (accommodative disposition) was accounted for by gender.

Two plausible explanations could be offered for the above result. First, that the influence of modernity may have leveled the gender field on role-play between men and women thereby making the traditional gender-role expectation a thing of the past. If the influence of modernity is tenable, then traditional views will begin to lose their influence and no more be the determinants of leadership qualification. Then competences, determined by the educational system, will replace traditional norms to give both male and female teachers equal pathways to headship positions. Second, it is possible, too, that either society is becoming all egalitarian or all traditionalist for some imperceptible reason, making the influence of gender an irrelevant factor in role-play and power ascription anymore. When every member of society thinks alike and expresses the same cultural views as to who qualifies to be a leader, the consideration of gender prerogative becomes an irrelevant and forgotten equation. Attitudes towards female heads may be the same as they will be towards male heads. Social distance toward a headmistress then may be the same as it will be towards a headmaster (male principal of a school).

However, as will be discussed in the next section, the significant association established by the results of this study between degree of egalitarianism and social distance (accommodative disposition) calls for a reexamination of the above possibilities and renders them untenable. Maybe, different studies need to be done in the future with different statistical techniques on the association between gender and social distance.

Degree of Egalitarianism and Social Distance

The degree of egalitarianism of teachers was found to be statistically significant in associating with teachers' social distance expressed in accommodative disposition. It was also found to be the strongest predictor among the other variables followed by teachers' age. Thus, the fourth and the sixth hypotheses of the study support earlier findings as revealed in the literature review. In response to the argument by scholars that discrimination or negative attitudes towards female heads is the natural response to society's lack of familiarity with women becoming leaders, Gazso (2004) insisted that the fundamental undercurrent to all gender-based discrimination (whether towards women or men), is the gender ideological beliefs of actors. This assertion of Gazso is supported by the results of this current study.

A similar assertion was made by Kroska and Elman (2009) when they investigated the effect of spouse's education, spouse's employment, spouse's gender ideological belief, spouse's religious service attendance, and the presence of a child 6 years and younger, on changes in husband's egalitarian feeling. Degree of egalitarianism emerged as the strongest predictor among other predictors. Also, in a cross-cultural investigation of attitudes towards women managers, Mostafa (2005) found similar results in United Arab Emirates sample. Gender ideological belief (patriarchy or traditionalism versus egalitarianism) emerged as one of the strongest correlates of attitudes towards women managers.

The predictive value of degree of egalitarianism or gender ideological beliefs, in general, on gender stereotypical discrimination has received extant research attention cross-culturally. These studies also found a strong correlation between the two variables. Thakathi and Lemmer (2002), from a South African sample of teachers and principals, for instance, investigated the role of degree of egalitarianism in predicting discrimination against female principals and found significant correlation between the two. This South African study also made an interesting observation about the age of the female principals in relation to discriminatory attitudes.

Gueye (2010), Skrla, Reyes, & Scheurich (2000), also concluded from their studies that in patriarchal societies, persons with traditional gender views become resentful anytime a female becomes their boss, and considered such a move as a threat to their normative cultural inheritance. This, they explained, was because men or women of such cultures hold less egalitarian views. In this study I argued that a breach of a cultural arrangement of male dominance and female subordination will constitute a *cold war* between egalitarians and traditionalists (less egalitarians). Such a conflict may breed resentments and lead to the creation of social distance between the female head and those who resent the breach of the cultural status quo of male hegemony. Coker, (2005) with others also alluded to such a conflict and the corollary behavioral response of social distancing.

The current study found a statistically significant association between degree of egalitarianism and teachers' social distance (accommodative disposition) with an inverse correlation. This means that teachers with less egalitarian views (traditional gender ideological views), tend to have greater social distance with their headmistresses, while teachers with higher degree of egalitarianism trade lesser social distance with their headmistresses. This finding refutes the assertion of Collard (2001) that gender ideological beliefs are no longer determinants of discriminatory attitudes towards women administrators. As Shapira, Arar, and Azaiza (2011) also recently observed, degree of egalitarianism is still a salient contributor to be considered in investigating gender-based discriminatory behaviors. The result of this current study emphasizes the fact that whatever the influence of modernity may be on todays' society, discrimination as a result of degree of egalitarianism still exists.

Interestingly, a remarkable observation is being made from this current study results: The mean age of the participants of this study was approximately 38 years. The oldest age of participants of the study was 75 years and the youngest age was 17 years. This puts the mean age of 38 into the middle-aged group. With a standard deviation of 10.94, indications are that, the sample comprised of a good number of young to mid-age teachers. If younger teachers demonstrated evidence of greater social distance as revealed by the study results, then, at least, the argument can be made that the future holds no prospects for a more egalitarian population of (younger) teachers.

This study, however, offers no support for the assertion that as older teachers retire and are replaced by younger generations of teachers, gender ideologically based discrimination then could be a thing of the past. This current finding compels me to concur with Shapira, Arar, and Azaiza (2011) that gender ideological beliefs still shape people's perception on the degree of social distance they are willing to have with persons of their out-group. This position is also shared by Bloom and Erlandson (2003); Foster, Amt, and Honkola, (2004).

The saliency of degree of egalitarianism as a prominent variable, among others, is therefore confirmed by this current study. Indeed, the degree of egalitarianism emerged as the strongest predictor of social distance among the four predictors (see Table 4.2). With a moderate effect, degree of egalitarianism accounted for 28 percent of variance in predicting teachers' social distance expressed in accommodative disposition.

Age and Social Distance

The age of teachers emerged as the second strongest predictor of teachers' social distance as expressed in accommodative disposition. The one most important study from which the fifth hypothesis derived was the Oduro and MacBeath's (2003) study. The Oduro and MacBeath's study found that older teachers (not younger teachers) were the most resentful of the authorities of their female heads and openly declared their resentment to these headmistresses. Since it was the older teachers (and not the younger ones) who most resented the female heads' authority, age therefore became an important variable of research concern in this study. As a result, age was propositioned as positively associating with teachers' social distance such that, younger teachers will show little or lesser social distance towards headmistresses of their schools.

Whereas the hypothesis of age-effect was supported by the test of statistical significance, the directionality of the association indicated an inverse correlation between the age and social distance variables. Consequently and contrary to my prediction, younger teachers did not show evidence of perceived lesser social distance with headmistresses as expected. Rather, the result revealed that the younger the teacher, the greater his or her social distance with the headmistress. This finding is not in line with the findings noted in the literature, where older teachers, because of their allegiance to the traditional gender views of male dominance, resented the authorities of female principals.

Because of the evidence in the current literature it would have made sense for older teachers to be less willing to trade interpersonal relationships with female heads of their schools. They (older teachers) should be the ones having wider or greater social distance with their headmistresses and not the younger teachers. It is, therefore, a little difficult explaining why younger teachers (rather than the older ones) tend to have greater or wider social distance with their headmistresses as found by this present study.

To understand this apparent anomaly, recourse to other aspects of the Ghanaian culture seems to offer hopes of plausible explanation of this revealed twist. We are reminded by Adjawodah and Beier (2004) and Geest (1997) that respect for authority is a serious moral value enshrined in the culture and traditions of the Ghanaian people.

According to Geest (1997), "Respect is the basic moral value which regulates social behavior. In its first, superficial, meaning it refers to a type of behavior which is shown, similar to etiquette or politeness" (p. 535). These scholars alluded to the fact that older people in Ghana hold on to this value (respect for old age and authority) more than the younger generations do. This may have explained why older teachers, in respect of the headmistress' authority as a leader, tended to be more accepting of her role as a leader, hence their willingness to establish interpersonal relationship (lesser social distance) with her. In this case then respect for authority (which was not investigated in this present study), may also have played an important role as degree of egalitarianism in determining teachers' social distance with their headmistress.

Another interesting phenomenon, found in a South African study, but which was not investigated in this study, may offer explanation to this twist of older (instead of younger teachers) expressing more egalitarian views and having lesser social distance with their headmistress. Thakathi and Lemmer (2002) reported that in South African, discrimination against female principals depends on how old the female principal is. They investigated the role of degree of egalitarianism in predicting discrimination against female principals and found that even though female principals suffered discrimination in this male dominated culture, the older the female principals, the less discriminated against they were. This meant that younger female principals suffered greater discrimination than older female principals in the South African study. Even though it is not clear why this is so, respect for old age, which is also a strong African cultural value, may have played some role in this trajectory.

In the Ghanaian culture, leaders, irrespective of their age, are considered elders and do enjoy the same respect that is accorded the elders of the community. Headmistresses as leaders automatically fall within the category of groups entitled to the honorary respect accorded elders. The older teachers understand this cultural expectation more than the younger generation of teachers. Even though respect as a construct was not measured in this study, it could be offering an explanation to why older teachers have better social distance with their headmistresses in this study than the younger teachers do. Respect then may have a heuristic value for future research.

As rightly noted by Geest (1997), respect for authority and old age is a serious cultural precept. I argue that since the elderly (more than the younger generation) are the chief adherents to traditional values, they are more likely to practice respect for authority than their younger counterparts. Respect, then, may be serving here as the undercurrent determining the accommodative disposition of the older teachers toward their headmistress. Even though respect is not being made here as synonymous with social distance (expressed in accommodative disposition), it may have served as the motivating force in determining teachers' social distance toward their headmistress.

Implications of the Study

The results of this study have several implications. First, using psycho-social variables such as the influence of gender ideological beliefs, the role of lineage ties, and perception of one's social distance in assessing degree of social interaction and cooperation with educational administrators is a rarity and novelty in sub-Saharan Ghana. For this current investigation, the extensive review of literature could not find any such study within the sub region to be replicated. Thus this new approach of taking a sociological look at issues of school administration does broaden the scope of research on school administrative issues and contributes immensely to the literature on school administration in Ghana and sub-Saharan Africa for that matter.

Second, from a methodological point of view, the use of multiple regression (MR) in the analyses, made it possible to test the individual contribution of each independent variable. This is a helpful deviation from the available qualitative studies and the few other studies using basic descriptive statistics in studying the administrative climate of schools in Ghana; this latter approach only results in limited theoretical models. This quantitative study however is a contribution also to the development of MR in studying interpersonal relationship between administrators and their subordinates and opens new grounds for future investigations. A replication of the MR study, using other models and designs, may lead to a better understanding of the problem being investigated here.

Third, findings of this study have made some revelations. The descriptive statistic revealed that more men (55.4 %) than women (44.6%) teach in the schools that were sampled for the study. Since some tertiary education is the minimum qualification for teachers to teach in the second cycle institutions of Ghana, the implications of the percentages are that the problem of gender disparity in the pursuit of higher education still pertains. Obviously then, the objective of the Girl-Child-Education (GCE) program in Ghana is yet to meet its goal. When Sutherland-Addy (2002 and Tanye (2008) discussed the issue of gender inequity in educational attainment in Ghana, their frustration, among others, was that the objective of the Girl-Child Education was long overdue. This calls for a step-up of the efforts at promoting girl-child education in Ghana. The GCE program must receive a boost from the Ministry of Education, the government of Ghana, and non-governmental organizations (NGOs) in Ghana.

Also, maybe it is about time a program of educational advancement campaign for women professionals is set up to encourage women to pursue in-service promotional courses that prepare and place them in administrative positions like their male counterparts. As more and more women qualify to assume principalship positions, familiarity with the rise of female leaders leveling the field of gender balance may change society's perception of females as inferior to males. That will give a fair tribute to the cry of gender inequity in the Ghanaian society on leadership prerogatives. The *modus operandi* for this educational advancement campaign may be through seminars and professional retreats for women at district and regional levels.

Conclusion

Probably, the most important finding of the study is the role *degree of egalitarianism* (gender ideological beliefs) played in determining teachers' social distance with their headmistresses. There is an inverse correlation between degree of egalitarianism and social distance of teachers with their female principals. Younger teachers were found to be less egalitarian and less willing to have close social distance with their headmistresses. Whether this study's finding is a true revelation of what is actually pertaining in the general Ghanaian society, cannot be ascertain here. A replication of this exploratory study of such a maiden territory needs to be done in order to find support that will lend credence to the actualities of such findings. However, if younger teachers of this study, in any shape or form, reflect what current Ghanaian society offers on the balance of egalitarian beliefs *vis a vis* attitudes towards women administrators, then cultural strands on gender ideological beliefs have very little to offer in the social distance discussion. The ramifications for this can be many and problematic to the ease of collaborative school administration.

At least for this study, the findings that, younger teachers were less egalitarian and thus have greater social distance with their headmistresses, revealed an inkling of discrimination on the part of younger teachers. The finding is indicative of the presence of resentment in younger teachers' disposition that caused them to socially distant themselves from their headmistress. The lack of good interpersonal relationship or lack of healthy social interaction between younger teachers and their headmistresses is recipe for noncooperation on the part of these younger teachers in the running of their school. It also has the potentials for conflict between teachers and their heads, and may cause apathy on the part of younger teachers. This could ultimately affect their performance as teachers in the classroom.

The administration of a school is a shared responsibility, which is not undertaken solely by the head alone but by all the stakeholders, including all teachers of the school building. There needs to be less (close) social distance (good interpersonal relationship) between teachers and their heads to ensure team work or what I will call here, *participatory administration.*

The point has been emphasized by scholars (Bogardus, 1971; Coker, 2005; Kambarami, 2006; Ko et al., 2006), that prejudices have potentials for discrimination thereby creating social distance between different subgroups. Evidence of discrimination between a superior and a subordinate in the school environment will not be a viable constituent of participatory administration. If the finding that gender ideological beliefs (degree of egalitarianism) do determine teachers' social distance with headmistresses is anything to go by, then something more than just the mere promotion of gender equity in the pursuit of higher education needs to be done.

It is the hope of this researcher that as more and more women teachers attain equal academic heights as their men counterparts, and as many more take up the mantel of school leadership, then male-biased gender orientation will begin to fade away. This could transform people's views on gender ideological beliefs and traditional gender roles between the sexes. The transformation of such tradition-long orientations could create a more egalitarian society. By the calculation of our current study, such re-orientation will improve interpersonal relationship between teachers and female heads of their school with positive ramifications for *participatory administration* of the Ghanaian schools.

Another interesting revelation made by this study contradicts what is known in the current literature and challenges our thinking about what may have caused younger teachers to have greater social distance towards their headmistress while the older teachers experience lesser social distance towards them. Indeed, the notion that modernity may have made the younger generation more egalitarian is undermined by this current finding. There is obviously, something about the crop of the younger teachers of this study that makes them have greater social distance with their headmistresses contrary to research expectation. Whatever that unexamined variable is that caused this unexpected correlation, was not accounted for in this study. Could it be the function of the moral decadence of Geest's (1997) assertion; where the culture of respect for authority is said to be waning away in the younger generation of Ghanaians? Or could it be due to the fact that the influence of gender ideological beliefs (degree of egalitarianism) is so strong, even in older generation of teachers, that the claim of modernity's influence for greater egalitarian disposition in the younger generation of teachers stands inconclusive?

There is the need for further investigation into why the younger generation of the teachers of our study has greater social distance than the older ones towards their headmistresses. This could be a systemic problem underlying this behavioral pattern as exhibited by the younger group of teachers and needs to be addressed by researchers and stakeholders of the education industry.

Limitations of the Study

The limitations of this study are mainly methodological. First, since no prior research exists in Ghana about the test of association among these study variables, this maiden research approach employed an exploratory research design for our analyses. Consequently, no causal relationships between study variables could be established. Results of the study, therefore, must not be treated as conclusive. Further research, with a true experimental design, needs to be undertaken and all possible explanations for the effects on the predicted variable(s) be controlled for before one can talk about causal relationship. This is not the case with this current study. In addition to the above, the data collection procedure was a nonprobability sampling strategy, which did not have a representative character of the targeted population. Results of the study therefore cannot be generalized for the population of teachers in second cycle institutions in Ghana. The results are limited to the sample studied.

The second limitation concerns the measurements used in this study. First, the SRES, a very reliable and commercially available instrument was used to measure degree of egalitarianism. This instrument was constructed for and adapted to the American western culture. In spite of its extensive use cross-culturally, it must be noted here that the semantic imports on some of the items on this instrument may not make sense to the Ghanaian participants. Phraseologies have different meanings from one culture to another and from one group of people to another. The items on the SRES are specifically constructed for the western culture. However, no adaptation to the sub-Saharan African culture was made of this instrument before administering it to the participating Ghanaian teachers. This could lead to measurement error should items on the instrument be answered incorrectly because they connote different meanings to participants. Even though there was no suspicion of such errors in this study, the likelihood of them is worth noting.

Third, the GSBD, which is a 10-item scale and measures teachers' social distance, is a new instrument. It was only tested in a pilot study by the researcher, who is also the author of it. It is worth noting that this is the first time the GSBDS is being used in a major study. A factor analysis of the GSBDS revealed two orthogonal subscales, which were named accommodative disposition scale and interpersonal affective disposition scale. Only 3 of the 10 items loaded on the latter scale while 7 loaded on the former. That the predictors of the study predicted the accommodative disposition but failed to predict the interpersonal affective disposition challenged the claim that the interpersonal affective disposition is a subscale of the social distance construct. What is likely is that the interpersonal affective disposition may not be measuring the domain of the social distance construct that it is purported to be measuring. Items on this scale may have been measuring something other than the social distance construct. This may explain why, for this sub-scale, there was no significant relationship found with any of the variables tested. A reevaluation of the scale items and their construct of measure is necessary for its future use.

Another weakness of this scale (Interpersonal affective disposition scale) lies in its reliability coefficient compared to the coefficient of accommodative disposition. Whereas the accommodative disposition has a reliability of .88, the reliability coefficient for the interpersonal affective disposition scale was .68, which was not strong enough. This also may have explained why it was not predicted in the study when the predictors were regressed on it.

Recommendations for Future Research

Since this was a cross-sectional analysis of study data, we could not manipulate the data for any causal inferences to be made of study results. Future research on behavioral pattern of teachers' social distance with headmistresses could benefit from a longitudinal research approach to see how behavior patterns evolve overtime. Also, a replication of this study with a revised GSBDS could produce different outcomes than current study findings.

Future research on the problem investigated here could also examine additional variables such as, the education of teachers, years of service, socio-economic status (SES), age of headmistresses, administrative style of headmistresses, respect for women, and the degree of egalitarianism of headmistresses themselves. This is because the administrative styles of headmistresses, for instance, could explain teacher-behavioral responses towards her and clarify reasons for the current associations among variables.

These limitations, notwithstanding, it is important to note that the current study has made an important contribution to the investigation of teachers' social distance with their headmistresses. At least for this maiden exploration of probable predictors of the construct, we know that degree of egalitarianism and age of teachers are important correlates of social distance towards headmistresses. Further research needs to examine these associations for a better understanding of the dynamics of interpersonal relationship, not only between teachers and their headmistresses, but also between subordinates and their women administrators in the greater society.

REFERENCES

Adjewodah, P., & Beier, P. (2004). *Working with traditional authority to conserve nature in West Africa.* Retrieved from http://www2.for.nau.edu/research/pb1/ Service/Adjewodah-Beier_Traditional_Authority_Conservation.pdf

Agboka, G. Y. (2006, March 20). *Some cultural practices in Ghana: Centuries behind in a modern society.* Retrieved from http://www.allAfrica.com

Agboli, M., Cutura, J., Ofusu-Amaah, A. W., Weeks, J., Gadzekpo, F., Amoako, B., & Kalenga, B. (2007, April). *Voices of women entrepreneurs in Ghana.* A report prepared by the IFC/World Bank Investment Climate Team for Africa in collaboration with IFC Gender Entrepreneurship Markets (GEM).

Aird, S. C. (n.d.). *Ghana's slaves to the gods: The custom of trokosi.* Retrieved from http://www.wcl.american.edu/hrbrief/v7il/ghana.htm

Alderfer, C. P., & Smith, K. K. (1982). Studying intergroup relations embedded in organizations. *Administrative Science Quarterly, 27,* 35-65.

Amancio, L. (2002). Gender and science in Portugal. *Portuguese Journal of Social Science, 1,* 185-199.

Ameh, R. K. (1998). Trokosi (child slavery) in Ghana: A policy approach. *The Journal of Ghana Studies Council, 1,* 35-62.

Amoakohene, M. I. (2004). Violence against women in Ghana: A look at women's perceptions and review of policy and social responses. *Social Science & Medicine, 59*, 2373-2385.

Amoako-Nuama, C. (1999). Changing *the culture*. Retrieved from http://www.unuep.org/ourplanet/imgversn/82/nuama.html

Amos-Wilson, P. M. (1999). Some issues concerning women in senior management: A case study from Ghana. *Public Administration and Development, 19*, 219-229.

Anderson, M. L. (1988). *Thinking about women: Sociological perspectives on sex and gender.* New York: McMillan Publishing Company.

Anderson, L. J. (2003). *Race, gender, and sexuality: Philosophical issues of identity and justice.* New Jersey: Prentice Hall.

Ardayfio-Schandorf, E. (2005, April 11-14). *Violence against women: The Ghanaian case.* Paper presented to the UN Division. Geneva, Switzerland.

Archer, R. (2002, April 22). Ghanaian women demand protection from violence. *The Ghanaian Chronicle.* Retrieved from http://www.un.org/ecosocdev/genifo/afrec/ vol15no4/154troko.htm

Avolio, B. J., Mhatre, K., Norman, S. M., & Lester, P. (2009). The moderating effect of gender on leadership intervention impact: An exploratory review. *Journal of Leadership & Organizational Studies, 15*, 325-341.

Awumbila, M. (2001). Women and gender equality in Ghana: A situational analysis. In D. Tsikata (Ed.), *Gender training in Ghana: Politics issues & tools* (pp. 33-50). Accra: Woeli Publishing Services.

Aryeetey, E. B. D. (2002). Behind the norms: women's access to land in Ghana In C. Toulmin, In P. L. Delville & S. Traore (Eds), *The dynamics of resource tenure in West Africa* (pp. 86-97). Oxford, UK, James Currey Ltd.

Bastick, T. (2001). *Influences on employment discrimination in the Caribbean: The case of the marginalized men and wasted women of Dominica.* (ERIC Document Reproduction Service No. ED460039).

Ben-Ari, N. (2001, December). Liberating girls from 'trokosi': Campaign against ritual servitude in Ghana. *Africa Recovery* [now called Africa Renewal], *15*, 26. Retrieved from http://www.un.org/ecosocdev/geninfo/afree/vol15no4/154troko.htm

Beere, C. A., King, D. W., Beere, D. B., & King, L. A. (1984). The Sex-Role Egalitarianism Scale: A measure of attitudes toward equality between the sexes. *Sex Roles, 10,* 563-576.

Bergmann, W. (1988). Attitude theory and prejudice In W. Bergmann *(Ed.), Error without trial: Psychological research on anti-Semitism* (pp. 271-301). New York: Walter de Gruyter & Co. Publishers.

Bernstein, M. J., Sacco, D. F., Young, S. G., Hugenberg, K., & Cook, E. (2010). Being "in" with the in-crowd: The effects of social exclusion and inclusion are enhanced by the perceived essentialism of ingroups and outgroups. *Personality and Social Psychology Bulletin, 36,* 999-1009.

Bloom, C., & Erlandson, D. A. (2003). African American women principals in urban schools: Realities, (re)constructions, and resolutions. *Educational Administration Quarterly, 39,* 339-369.

Blumer, H. (1937). Social psychology. In E. P. Schmidt (Ed.), *Man and society: A substantive introduction to the social sciences* (pp. 144–198). New York: Prentice Hall.

Bogardus, E. S. (1922). *A history of social thought.* Los Angeles: University of Southern California Press.

Bogardus, E. S. (1925). Social distance and its origins. *Sociology and Social Research, 9,* 216-225.

Bogardus, E. S. (1933). A social distance scale. *Sociology and Social Research, 22*, 265-271.

Bogardus, E. S. (1947). Measurement of personal-group relations. *Sociometry, 10*, 306-311.

Bogardus, E. S. (1947). Changes in racial distance. *International Journal of Attitude and Opinion Research, 1*, 55-62.

Bogardus, E. S. (1958). Racial distance changes in the United States during the past thirty years. *Sociology and Social Research, 43*, 127-135.

Bogardus, E. S. (1959). *Social distance.* Yellow Springs, OH: Antioch Press.

Bogardus, E. S. (1967). *A forty-year racial distance study.* Los Angeles: University of Southern California Press.

Bogardus, E. S. (1968). Comparing racial distance in Ethiopia, South Africa, and the United States. *Sociology and Social Research, 52*, 149-156.

Bogardus, E. S. (1971). *The Mexican in the United States.* Los Angeles: University of Southern California Press.

Bohmig, C. (2010). *Ghanaian nurses at a crossroads: Managing expectations on a medical ward.* Retrieved from http://dare.uva.nl/document/163560.

Briles, J. (1999). *Woman to woman 2000: Becoming sabotage savvy in the new millennium.* Far Hills, NJ: New Horizon Press.

Bryman. A., & Cramer. D. (2009). *Quantitative data analysis with SPSS 14, 15, & 16: A guide for social scientists.* New York: Routledge Taylor & Francis Group.

Bryson, D. (2009). Personality and culture, the social science research council, and liberal social engineering: The advisory committee on personality and culture, 1930-1934. *Journal of the History of the Behavioral Sciences, 45,* 355-386.

Buchan, N., & Croson, R. (2004). The boundaries of trust: Own and others' actions in the US and China. *Journal of Economic Behavior & Organization, 55,* 485-504.

Byrne, D., & Kiger, G. (1988). Contemporary measure of attitudes toward blacks. *Educational and Psychological Measurement, 48,* 107-118. doi: 10.1177/001316448804800113

Chao, S. (Ed.). (1999). *Ghana: Gender analysis and policymaking for development* –World Bank discussion paper No. 403, Washington, D.C. Retrieved from http://go.worldbank.org/05VVG6LC20

Coker, E. (2005). Selfhood and social distance: Toward a cultural understanding of psychiatric stigma in Egypt. *Social Science & Medicine, 61,* 920-930.

Cohen, J. (1988). *Statistical power analysis for the behavioral science* (2nd ed.). Hillsdale, NJ: Lawrence Erlbaum Associates.

Collard, J. (2001). Leadership and gender: An Australian perspective. *Educational Management and Administration, 29,* 343-355.

Coltrane, S. (2001). Marketing the marriage "solution": Misplaced simplicity in the politics of fatherhood. *Sociological Perspectives, 44,* 387-418.

Costello, A. B., & Osborne, J. W. (2005). Best practices in exploratory factor analysis: Four recommendations for getting the most from your analysis. *Practical Assessment, Research & Evaluation, 10,* 1-9. Retrieved from http://pareonline.net/getyn.asp?v=10&n=7

Cox, T. H., & Nkomo, S. M. (1993). Race and ethnicity. In R. Golembiewski (Ed.), *Handbook of organization behavior* (pp. 205-230). New York: Marcel Dekker.

Christman, D., & McClellan, R. (2008). "Living on barbed wire": Resilient women administrators in educational leadership programs. *Educational Administration Quarterly, 44,* 3-29.

DeCoster, J., & Claypool, H. (2004). *Data analysis in SPSS.* Retrieved from http://www.stat-help.com/notes.html

Devika, J. (2006). Negotiating women's social space: Public debates on gender in early modern Kerala, India. *Inter-Asia Cultural Studies, 7,* 43-61.

Diekman, A. B., & Hirnisey, L. (2007). The effect of context on the silver ceiling: A role congruity perspective on prejudiced responses. *Personality and Social Psychology Bulletin, 33,* 1353-1366.

Ding, C., & Hershberger, S. (2002). Assessing content validity and content equivalence using structural equation modeling. *Structural Equation Modeling, 9,* 283-297.

Etter-Lewis, G. (2000). Spellbound: Audience, identity and self in black women's narrative discourse. In T. Cosslett, C. Lury, & P. Summerfield (Eds.), *Feminism and autobiography: Texts, theories, methods* (pp. 107-128). New York: Routledge.

Fagenson, E. A. (Ed.). (1993). *Women in management: Trends, issues, and challenges in managerial diversity.* Newbury Park, CA: Sage Publications.

Fennell, H. (1997). Power in the principalship: Four women's experiences. *Journal of Educational Administration, 37,* 23-49.

Forson, C. (2007). *Systems theory, test of quality, and school effectiveness in Ghana.* Unpublished dissertation. St. John University, New York.

Foster, M. D., Arnt, S., & Honkola, J. (2004). When the advantaged become disadvantaged: Men's and women's actions against gender discrimination. *Sex Roles, 50,* 27-36.

Fowler, F. J., (1993). *Survey research methods* (2nd ed.). Newbury Park: Sage Publications.

Frick, W. C. (2008). Principals' value-informed decision making, intrapersonal moral discord, and pathways to resolution: the complexities of moral leadership praxis. *Journal of Educational Administration, 47,* 50-74.

Friedrich-Ebert-Stiftung, & Allah-Mensah, B. (2005). *Women in politics and public life I Ghana.* Accra: Friedrich-Ebert-Foundation.

Funk, C. (2002). *Gender equity in educational institutions: Problems, practices, and strategies for change.* (ERIC Document Reproduction Service No. ED 476601).

Gall, M. D., Gall, J. P., & Borg, W. R. (2010). *Applying educational research: How to read, do, and use research to solve problems of practice* (6th ed.). Boston: Pearson.

Gazso, A. (2005). Gendering the vertical mosaic: Feminist perspectives on Canadian society (review). *The Canadian Journal of Sociology, 30,* 376-379.

Gedzi, V. (2009, June). *Women and property inheritance after intestate succession, Law 111 in Ghana.* A paper presented at IAFFE Conference, Boston.

Gender equality and social institutions in Ghana. (2008). *Ghana living standards survey report of the fifth round (GLSS 5).* Accra: Ghana Statistical Service.

George, D., & Mallery, P. (2011). *SPSS for windows step by step: A simple guide and reference.* Boston: Allyn & Bacon.

Geest, S. (1997). Money and respect: The changing values of old age in rural Ghana. *Africa, 67,* 534-559.

Ghana Education Service: Secondary education division – addresses of secondary schools 2004/2005. Available at the Man Power Division of Ministry of Education (Headquarters, Ministries, Accra).

Giannopoulos, C., Conway, M., & Mendelson, M. (2005). The gender of status: The laypersons' perception of status groups is gender-typed. *Sex Roles, 53,* 795-806.

Gibbons, J. L., Hamby, B. A., & Dennis, W. D. (1997). Researching gender-role ideologies internationally and cross-culturally. *Psychology of Women Quarterly, 21,* 151-170.

Gueye, K. (2010). "Tyrannical femininity" in Nawal El Saadawi's memoirs of a woman doctor. *Research in African Literatures, 41,* 160-172.

Hargens, L. L., & Long, S. J. (2002). Demographic inertia and women's representation among faculty in higher education. *The Journal of Higher Education, 73,* 494-517.

Heise, D. R. (1970). The semantic differential and attitude research. In G. F. Summers (Ed.), *Attitude measurement* (pp. 235-253). Chicago, IL: Rand McNally.

Herek, G. M., & Capitanio, J. P. (1996). "Some of my best friends": Intergroup contact, concealable stigma, and heterosexuals' attitude towards gay men and lesbians. *Personality and Social Psychology Bulletin, 22,* 412-424.

Hofstede, G., & McCrae. R. R., (2004). Personality and culture revisited: Linking traits and dimensions of culture. *Cross-Cultural Research, 38,* 52-88.

Honeck, S. M. (1981). *An exploratory study of the Beere-King Sex-Role Egalitarianism Scale, the MacDonald Sex Role Survey, and Spence and Helmreich's Attitudes Toward Women Scale.* Unpublished master's thesis, Central Michigan University, Pleasant MI.

Horowitz, L., (2009). *Getting good government for women: a literature review.* A document of The International Bank for Reconstruction and Development/The World Bank. Retrieved from http://siteresources.worldbank.org/EXTARD/Resources/336681-1220903855412/GenderandGovernanceLitReview.pdf

Hoy, W. K., & Tarter, C. J. (1995). Administrators solving the problems of practice: Decision-making concepts, cases, and consequences. Boston: Allyn & Bacon.

Interstate Succession Act, 1985 (PNDCL 111), Ghana.

Jaffa, M. (1985). [Administration of Sex-Role Egalitarianism Scale and Attitude Towards Women Scale]. Unpublished raw data, Central Michigan University, Pleasant, MI.

Jalava, J. (2003). From norms to trust: The Luhmannian connections between trust and system. *European Journal of Social Theory, 6,* 173-190.

Kambarami, M. (2006). *Femininity, sexuality and culture: Patriarchy and female subordination in Zimbabwe.* South Africa & University of Fort Hare: African Regional Sexuality Resource Centre. Retrieved from http://www.hst.org.za

Kannae, L. A. (1993). *The masculine side of family planning: Male government employees' attitudes and use of family planning methods in Ghana.* Unpublished dissertation, The University of Akron, Akron, Ohio.

Katenbrink, J. (2006). Translation and standardization of the sex-role egalitarianism scale (SRES-B) on a German sample. *Sex Roles, 54,* 485-493.

Keshet, S., Kark, R., Pomerantz-Zorin, L., Koslowsky, M., & Schwarzwald, J. (2006). Gender, status and the use of power strategies. *European Journal of Social Psychology, 36,* 105-117.

King, R. (2006 *January-March*). Is it time for a progress report on violence against women in Ghana? *Human Rights Review,* 75-97.

King, L. A., Beere, D. B., King, D. W., & Beere, C. A. (1984). *Validity data on the sex-role egalitarianism scale.* Unpublished raw data, Central Michigan University.

King, L. A., & King, D. W. (1997). Sex-Role Egalitarianism Scale: Development, psychometric properties, and recommendations for future. *Psychology of Women Quarterly, 21,* 71-87.

King, L. A., King, D. W., Carter, D. B., Surface, C. R., & Stepanski, K. (1994). Validity of the Sex-Role Egalitarianism Scale: Two replication studies. *Sex Roles, 31,* 339-348.

Kise, J. A. G., & Russell, B. (2008). *Differentiated school leadership: Effective collaboration, communication, and change through personality type.* Thousand Oaks, CA: Sage Publication Company.

Ko, S. J., Judd, C. M., & Blair, I. V. (2006). What the voice reveals: Within- and between-category stereotyping on the basis of voice. *Personality and Social Psychology Bulletin, 32,* 806-819.

Ko, S. J., Judd, C. M., & Stapel, D. A. (2009). Stereotyping based on voice in the presence of individuating information: Vocal femininity affects perceived competence but not warmth. *Personality and Social Psychology Bulletin, 35,* 198-211.

Koivunen, J. M., Rothaupt, J. W., & Wolfgram, S. M. (2009). Gender dynamics and role adjustment during the transition to parenthood: Current perspectives. *The Family Journal, 17,* 323-328.

Koslowsky, M., Schwarzwald, J., & Ashuri, S. (2001). On the relationship between subordinates' compliance to power sources and organizational attitudes. *Applied Psychology: An International Review, 50,* 455-476.

Krieglmeyer, R., De Houwer, J., & Deutsch, R. (2011). How farsighted are behavioral tendencies of approach and avoidance? The effect of stimulus valence on immediate vs. ultimate distance change. *Journal of Experimental Social Psychology, 47,* 622-627.

Kroska, A., & Elman, C. (2009). Change in attitude about employed mothers: exposure, interests, and gender ideology discrepancies. *Social Science Research, 38,* 366-382.

Langer, G. (2003, May/June). About response rate: Some unresolved questions. *Public Perspective.* Retrieved from http://www.aapor.org/Content/ NavigationMenu/ PollampSurveyFAQs/DoResponseRatesMatteR/ Response_Rates_-_Langer.pdf

Lee, M. Y., Sapp, S. G, & Ray, M. C. (1996). The reverse social distance scale. *The Journal of Social Psychology, 136,* 17-24.

Leech, N., Barrett, K., & Morgan, G. (2005). *SPSS for intermediate statistics: Use and interpretation* (2nd ed). Mahwah, NJ: Lawrence Erlbaum Associates.

Lobel, T., Mashraki-Pedhatzur, S., Mantzur, A., & Libby, S. (2000). Gender discrimination as a function of stereotypic and counter stereotypic behavior: a cross-cultural study. *Sex Roles: A Journal of Research, 43,* 395-406.

Lemon, N. (1973). *Attitudes and their measurement.* New York: John Wiley & Sons.

Li, H. (2002). Culture, gender and self-close-other(s) connectedness in Canadian and Chinese samples. *European Journal of Social Psychology, 32,* 93-104.

Loder, T. (2005). On deferred dreams, callings, and revolving doors of opportunity: African-American women's reflections on becoming principals. *The Urban Review, 37,* 243-265.

Lorier, A. (2008). *Sex slaves to the gods? Do you care?* Retrieved from www. associatedcontent.com/article/543423/child_sex_slaves_to_the_gods_do_you_pg3.html?cat=38

Lynch, M., & McConatha, D. (2006). Hyper-symbolic interactionism: Prelude to a refurbished theory of symbolic interaction or just old wine? *Sociological Viewpoints, 22,* 87-96.

MacInnes, J. (1998). Analysing patriarch capitalism and women's employment in Europe. *Innovation: The European Journal of Social Sciences, 11,* 227-248.

Marshall, C. (2004). Social justice challenges to educational administration: Introduction to a special issue. *Educational Administration Quarterly, 40,* 3-13.

McGhee, M. R., Johnson, N., & Liverpool, J. (2002). Assessing psychometric properties of the Sex-Role Egalitarianism Scale (SRES) with African Americans. *Sex Roles, 45,* 859-866.

McHugh, M. C., & Frieze, I. H. (1997). The measurement of gender-role attitudes: a review and commentary. *Psychology of Women Quarterly, 21,* 1-16.

McNeil, K., Newman, I., & Kelly, F. (1996). *Testing research hypotheses with the general linear model.* Carbondale: Southern Illinois University Press.

Meier, K., & Wilkins, V. (2002). Gender differences in agency head salaries: The case of public education. *Public Administration Review, 62,* 405-411.

Mertler, A. C., & Vannatta, A. R. (2010). *Advanced and multivariate statistical methods: Practical application and interpretation* (4th ed.). Glendale, CA: Pyrczak Publishing.

Meyer, H. A., Astor, R. A., & Behre, W. J. (2002). Teachers' reasoning about school violence: the role of gender and location. *Contemporary Educational Psychology, 27,* 499-528.

Minkah-Premo, Y. N. S. (2001). *Coping with violence against women.* Accra, Ghana: Asempa Publishers.

Minkah-Premo, S., & Dowuona-Hammond, C. (2005). *Recommendations for integrating gender issues into the land administration project: Review of land and gender studies and identification of resources in Ghana.* Ghana Land Administration Project. Research Report (unpublished).

Mostafa, M. M. (2005). Attitudes towards women managers in the United Arab Emirates: The effects of patriarchy, age, and sex differences. *Journal of Managerial Psychology, 20,* 522-540.

Mueller, D. (1986). *Measuring social attitudes: A handbook for researchers and practitioners.* New York: Teachers College Press.

Newman, I., Newman, C., Brown, R., & McNeely, S. (2006). *Conceptual statistics for beginners* (3rd ed.). New York: University Press of America.

Nukunya, G. (1992). *Tradition and change in Ghana: An introduction to sociology.* Accra, Ghana: Ghana University Press.

Nukunya, G. (1987). *Social structure of Ghana.* Lecture notes, Department of sociology, University of Ghana, Legon, Accra, Ghana.

Odell, P., Korgen, K., & Wang, G. (2005). Cross-racial friendships and social distance between racial groups on a college campus. *Innovative Higher Education, 29,* 291-305.

Oduro, G. K., & Macbeath, J. (2003). Traditions and tensions in leadership: the Ghanaian experience. *Cambridge Journal of Education, 33,* 441-455.

Ofei-Aboagye, R. (1994). Altering the strands of the fabric: A preliminary look at domestic violence in Ghana. Signs: *Journal of Women in Culture and Society, 119*, 925-938.

Ofori, S. (2008). *A reflection on the matrimonial property rights in Ghana: Is marriage a bar to the acquisition of wealth?* Unpublished paper.

Oishi, S. (2004). Personality in culture: A neo-Allportian view. *Journal of Research in Personality, 38*, 68-74.

Osmond, M. W., & Thorne, B. (1993). The social construction of gender in families and society. In P. G. Boss, W. J. Doherty, R. LaRossa, W. R. Schumm, & S. K. Steinmetz (Eds.), *Sourcebook of family theories and methods: A contextual approach* (pp. 591-625). New York: Springer Publishing.

Owusu-Ansah, A. (2003). Trokosi in Ghana: Cultural relativism or slavery? The African Symposium. *Online Journal of African Educational Research, 3*(4). Retrieved from http://www.ncsu.edu/ncsu/aern/symposium_main.htm

Parrillo, V., & Donoghue, C. (2005). Updating the Bogardus social distance studies: A new national survey. *The Social Science Journal, 42*, 257-271.

Peters, P. E. (2010). Contesting land and custom in Ghana. State, chief and the citizen. *Journal of Agrarian Change, 10*,106-608.

Plant, A. E., Kling, K. C., & Smith, G. L. (2004). The influence of gender and social role on the interpretation of facial expressions. *Sex Roles, 51*, 187-196.

Polit, F. D., & Beck, T. C. (2006). The content validity index: Are you sure you know what's being reported? Critique and recommendations. *Research in Nursing & Health, 29*, 489-497.

Popham. J. W. (1978). *Criterion-referenced measurement*. Englewood Cliffs, NJ: Prentice Hall.

Qian, Z. (2002). Race and social distance: intermarriage with non-Latino Whites. *Race & Society, 5,* 33-47.

Quisumbing, A., Payongayong, E., Aidoo, J. B., & Otsuka, K. (1999). Women's land rights in transition to individualized ownership: Implications for the management of tree resources in West Africa. *FCND Discussion Paper, No. 58.* (International Food Policy Research Institute).

Randall, N. H., & Delbridge, S. (2005). Perceptions of social distance in an ethnically fluid community. *Sociological Spectrum, 25,* 103-122.

Rashotte, L. S., & Webster, M. (2005). Gender status beliefs. *Social Science Research, 34,* 618-633.

Riek, B. M., Mania, E. W., & Gaertner, S. L. (2006). Intergroup threat and outgroup attitudes: A meta-analytic review. *Personality and Social Psychology Review, 10,* 336-353.

Rinaudo, B. (2003). *Trokosi slavery: Injustice in the name of religion*. African Studies Association of Australasia and the Pacific 2003 Conference Procedings – African on Global Stage. La Trobe University.

Rokeach, M. (1961). Belief versus race as determinants of social distance: Comment on Triandis' paper. *Journal of Abnormal and Social Psychology, 62,* 187-188.

Rosenbaum, T. (2009). Applying theories of social exchange and symbolic interaction in the treatment of unconsummated marriage/relationship. *Sexual & Relationship Therapy, 24,* 38-46.

Rundquist, T. J. (1996, March). *Racial attitude survey*. State Big Rapids, MI: Nova Media.

Runger, M. (2006). *Governance, land rights and access to land in Ghana: A development perspective on gender equity.* Paper presented at the 5th FIG Regional Conference in Accra, Ghana [March 8-11, 2006].

Russo, N. F. (1997). Forging new directions gender role measurement (editorial). *Psychology of Women Quarterly, 21,* i-ii.

Selby, H. (2008, June 22). *Ghana: Inhumane aspects of cultural practices.* Retrieved from http://www.allAfrica.com

Scandura, T., Tejeda, M. J., & Lankau, M. J. (1995). An examination of the validity of the sex-role egalitarianism scale (SRES-KK) using confirmatory factor analysis procedures. *Educational and Psychological Measurement, 55,* 832-840.

Shapira, T., Arar, K., & Azaiza, F. (2010). Arab women principals' empowerment and leadership in Israel. *Journal of Educational Administration, 48,* 704-715.

Shum, L. C., & Cheng, Y. C. (1997). Perception of women principals' leadership and teachers' work attitude. *Journal of Educational Administration, 35,* 165-184.

Simon, S. (2008). What's a good value for Cronbach's alpha? Retrieved from http://www.childrensmercy.org/stats/weblog2004/CronbachAlpha.asp

Skrla, L., Reyes, P., & Scheurich, J. J. (2000). Sexism, silence, and solutions: Women superintendents speak up and speak out. *Educational Administration Quarterly, 36,* 44-75.

Sossou, M. (2006). *The meaning of gender equality in Ghana: Women's perceptions of the issues of gender equality: implications for social work education and practice in Ghana. Women in Welfare Education.* Retrieved from www.thefreelibrary.com/ print/PrintArticle.aspx?id=165971629

Stephens, D. (2000). Girls and basic education in Ghana: A cultural enquiry. *International Journal of Educational Development, 20,* 29-47.

Stevens, J. P. (1996). *Applied multivariate statistics for the social sciences* (3rd ed.). Hillsdale, NJ: Erlbaum.

Stevens, J. P. (2002). *Applied multivariate statistics for the social sciences* (4th ed.). Hillsdale, NJ: Erlbaum.

Stith, S. M. (1986). *Police officer response to marital violence predicted from the officer's attitudes, stress, and marital experience: A path analysis.* Unpublished doctoral dissertation, Kansas State University.

Sugarman, D., & Frankel, S. (1996). Patriarchal ideology and wife-assault: A meta-analytic review. *Journal of Family Violence, 11,* 13-40.

Sutherland-Addy, E. (2002). Impact assessment study of the girls' education programme in Ghana. *A Report for UNICEF-Ghana.*

Tabachnick, B. G., & Fidell, L. S. (2001). *Using multivariate statistics* (4th ed.). Boston, MA: Allyn & Bacon.

Takyi, B. K., & Broughton, C. (2006). Marital stability in sub-Saharan Africa: Do women's autonomy and socioeconomic situation matter? *Journal of Family and Economic Issues, 27,* 113-132.

Takyi, B. K., & Gyimah, S. O. (2007). Matrilineal family ties and marital dissolution in Ghana. *Journal of Family Issues, 28,* 682-705.

Takyi, B. K., & Addai, I. (2002). Religious affiliation, marital processes and women's educational attainment in a developing society. *Sociology of Religion, 63,* 177-193.

Tang, K. (2004). Internationalizing women's struggle against discrimination: The UN women's conversion and the optional protocol. *British Journal of Social Work, 34,* 1173-1188.

Tanye, M. (2008). Access and barriers to education for Ghanaian women and girls. *Interchange, 39,* 167-184.

Thakathi, T., & Lemmer, E. M. (2002). Community strategies of women in educational management. *South African Journal of Education, 22,* 193-197.

Triandis, H. C., & Davis, E. E. (1965). Race and belief as determinants of behavioral intentions. *Journal of Personality and Social Psychology, 2,* 715-725.

Triandis, H. C. (1971). *Attitude and attitude change.* New York: John Wiley & Sons.

Triandis, H., & Triandis, L. (1988). Race, social, religion, and nationality as determinants of social distance. In W. Bergmann (Ed.), *Error without trial* (pp. 501-516). New York: Walter de Gruyter & Co.

Triandis, H. C., & Gelfand, M. J. (1998). Converging measurement of horizontal and vertical individualism and collectivism. *Journal of Personality and Social Psychology, 74,* 118-128.

Tsikata, D. (1997). *Women, land tenure and inheritance in Ghana: Equal Access or discrimination?* Retrieved from http://www.gwsafrica.org/ knowledge/ dzodzi.html

Tyler, T., Huo, Y., & Lind, A. E. (2000). Cultural values and authority relations: the psychology of conflict resolution across cultures. *Psychology, Public Policy and Law, 6,* 1138-1163.

Ui, M., & Matsui, Y. (2008). Japanese adults' sex role attitudes and judgment criteria concerning gender equality: The diversity of gender egalitarianism. *Sex Roles, 58*, 412-422.

Vedlitz, A., & Zahran, S. (2007). Theories of ethnic social distance: Comparative empirical tests for three distinct ethnic groups. *Sociological Spectrum, 27,* 585-603.

Walsh, A. (1990). *Statistics for the social sciences: With computer applications.* New York: Harper & Row Publishers.

Walz., C. F., Strickland, O. L., & Lenz., E. R. (2005). *Measurement in nursing and health research* (3rd ed.). New York: Springer Publishing Co.

Wark, C., & Galliher, J. (2007). Emory Bogardus and the origins of the social distance scale. *The American Sociologist, 38,* 383-295.

Weaver, C. (2008). Social distance as a measure of prejudice among ethnic groups in the United States. *Journal of Applied Social Psychology, 38,* 779-795.

Williamson, R. (1976). Social distance and ethnicity: Some subcultural factors among high school students. *Urban Education, XI,* 295-312.

Whitehead, A., & Tsikata, D. (2003). Policy discourse on women's land rights in sub-Saharan Africa: The implications of the Re-turn to the customary. *Journal of Agrarian Change, 3,* 67-112.

World Bank Group of International Finance Corporation. (2007). *Voices of women entrepreneurs in Ghana.* [A Report prepared by the IFC/World Bank Investment Climate Team for Africa in collaboration with IFC Gender Entrepreneurship Markets (GEM)], Johannesburg: South Africa.

Women's Manifesto by Abantu for Development, Ghana. (2004). *Actual women situation in Ghana* [WiLDAF/FeDDAF]. Retrieved from http://www.wildaf-ao.org/eng/spip.php?page=print_articles&id_article=43

Zafarullah, H. (2000). Through the brick wall, and the glass ceiling women in the civil service in Bangladesh. *Gender, Work and Organization, 7,* 197-209.

APPENDICES

APPENDIX A

FINAL COPY OF THE GHANA SPECIFIC BEHAVIORAL DIFFERENTIAL SCALE (GSBDS): SPECIFIC INSTRUCTION FOR RESPONDENTS

In every society like ours, people relate with one another based on the degree of social ties existing between them or because of common values or interest, which they share together. The relationship between a superior and a subordinate is different from the one between two siblings, or close relations. Superiors are respected, honored, and obeyed because of the position they occupy. People's attitude towards their superiors, however, is determined by whether or not the superiors are seen as good fits for the positions they occupy. There is respect for those who are judged as capable of the demand of their offices and suspicion and disrespect for those judged as misfits for their positions.

This booklet contains statements about your female principal. For each item on the scale, rate your feelings toward your **principal** as an **administrator.** There are no right or wrong answers. Also, some of the items seem to make more sense than others. **Do not** worry about that. Just rate the extent to which you agree or not agree with the statement.

Please do not leave any item blank. The information you provide here is strictly confidential. The data will only be used for research purposes. Please feel free to give your personal opinion in responding to these statements.

Please check or write in the space provided what applies to you.

Gender: Male (   ) Female (   )

Lineage System: Patrilineal (   ) Matrilineal (   )

Age: (Please print) _____

Now respond to the following statements using a check mark to indicate how much you agree or disagree with the statement. For example, check marks toward the left indicate your agreement with the response on the left and check marks towards the right indicate your agreement with the response on the right. The closer your check mark is to a particular response, the stronger your degree of agreement with that particular response. The further away your check mark is from a statement the more your disagreement with that statement.

THE WOMAN PRINCIPAL/HEADMISTRESS OF MY SCHOOL:

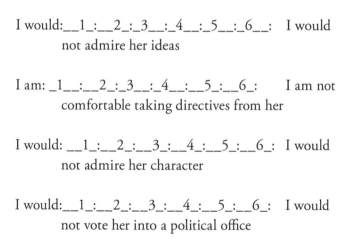

I would:__1_:__2_:_3__:_4__:_5__:_6__: I would
　　　　not admire her ideas

I am: _1__:__2_:_3__:_4__:__5_:__6_: I am not
　　　　comfortable taking directives from her

I would: __1_:__2_:__3_:_4_:__5_:__6_: I would
　　　　not admire her character

I would:__1_:__2_:__3_:__4_:__5_:__6_: I would
　　　　not vote her into a political office

I would:__1_:__2_:__3_:__4_:__5_:__6_: I would
        not gossip with her

I would:__1_:__2_:__3_:__4_:__5_:__6_: I would
        not accept her as an intimate friend

I would:__1_:__2_:__3_:__4_:__5_:__6_: I would
        not support her promotion

I would:__1_:__2_:__3_:__4_:__5_:__6_: I would
        not confide my secrets in her

I would:__1_;__2_:__3_:__4_:__5_:__6_: I would
        not defend her rights if they were jeopardized

I would:__1_:__2_:__3_:__4_:__5_:__6_: would
        not have as my mentor

APPENDIX B

IRB APPROVAL

NOTICE OF APPROVAL

Date: August 11, 2008

To: Patrick Allala
PO Box 13824
Fairlawn, Ohio 44334

From: Sharon McWhorter, IRB Administrator

Re: IRB Number 20060804-3
"*Multivariate Analysis of Teachers' Attitude toward Female Principals in the Ghanaian Male-Chauvinistic Society: A Gender Ideological Investigation*"

Thank you for submitting your Application for Continuing Review of Research Involving Human Subjects for the referenced project. Your protocol represents minimal risk to subjects and has been approved under Expedited Category #7.

Approval Date: August 11, 2008
Expiration Date: August 21, 2009
Continuation Application Due: August 7, 2009

In addition, the following is/are approved:

☐ Waiver of documentation of consent
☒ Waiver or alteration of consent
☐ Research involving children
☐ Research involving prisoners

Please adhere to the following IRB policies:

- IRB approval is given for not more than 12 months. If your project will be active for longer than one year, it is your responsibility to submit a continuation application prior to the expiration date. We request submission two weeks prior to expiration to insure sufficient time for review.
- A copy of the approved consent form must be submitted with any continuation application.
- If you plan to make any changes to the approved protocol you must submit a continuation application for change and it must be approved by the IRB before being implemented.
- Any adverse reactions/incidents must be reported immediately to the IRB.
- If this research is being conducted for a master's thesis or doctoral dissertation, you must file a copy of this letter with the thesis or dissertation.
- When your project terminates you must submit a Final Report Form in order to close your IRB file.

Additional information and all IRB forms can be accessed on the IRB web site at:
http://www.uakron.edu/research/orssp/compliance/IRBHome.php

☒ Approved consent form/s enclosed

Cc: Susan Olson- Advisor
Cc: Rosalie Hall - IRB Chair

Office of Research Services and Sponsored Programs
Akron, OH 44325-2102
330-972-7666 • 330-972-6281 Fax

The University of Akron is an Equal Education and Employment Institution

APPENDIX C

LETTER TO THE PRINCIPALS

Dear Principal,

<u>PERMISSION TO CONDUCT SURVEY IN YOUR SCHOOL</u>

I, the undersigned, Patrick N. Allala, a doctoral student of the University of Akron in Akron, Ohio, U.S.A., wish to undertake a survey in your school on teachers' attitude toward female principals in the Ghanaian male chauvinistic society. Information gathered from this survey will form part of the data needed for the completion of my doctoral dissertation.

Your permission is kindly requested to allow teachers from your school to participate in the survey. The selection of your school was a result of a carefully chosen sample for this study.

The analysis of the information collected from teachers, should help us address some of the current concerns about discrimination against women, especially female superiors, at workplaces within the sub-region.

Given the nature of the survey, it is highly advised that principals be not involved in the survey nor be present during the process. This is to ensure that teachers feel comfortable enough to freely express their feelings without any external intimidation or fear that may result from your presence around the survey area.

May I also request for the availability of a common room for all teachers, where the investigator (the person who conducts the survey) will instruct willing participants about the conduct of the survey.

Information from the survey is confidential and will be used only for purposes of the research. In this study there will be no mention of names of participants or participating schools. This is to emphasize the confidential character of the study.

The principal investigator will contact you by phone or in person (if practicable) to discuss the date and the necessary arrangements for the survey. Please kindly give him/her all the support needed for a smooth exercise. Your cooperation is highly appreciated.

If there is any question or concern, please do not hesitate to contact me either by email: nikypee@neo.rr.com or by phone: 330-475-5866.

Thanks for your anticipated cooperation.

Sincerely yours,

Patrick N. Allala (Rev. Fr.)

APPENDIX D

APPROVED GENERAL INSTRUCTION FOR TEACHERS/PARTICIPANTS

GENERAL INSTRUCTION FOR TEACHERS/PARTICIPANTS

Ladies and gentlemen,

We want to thank you very much for your participation in this important survey. You will be handed some questionnaires that ask you personal questions to which you are expected to give your private opinion and not what you think represents others' opinions. You are the only person who knows what your responses are. You are not to share these responses with anybody before, during, or after the survey. Data collected from this survey will be treated highly confidential and shall be used only for research purposes. Hence, you should not identify yourself by name on the questionnaire.

There will be two separate questionnaires to respond to. In order to match these questionnaires to respondents, each teacher will be assigned a number chosen randomly. Write your number at the top right corner of your questionnaires. For example, if teacher A's number is 13, teacher A will write "13" on both papers. This will help the investigator identify which questionnaires have been answered by teacher A.

Questionnaires will be coded. This will make it possible for accurate follow-up to obtain questionnaires from non-responding individuals. Principals are not allowed around the area of the survey nor will they be involved in any part of the process. You are therefore, encouraged to freely respond to the questions according to how you truly feel about the statements on the scale.

Thanks for your cooperation.

APPROVED
AUG 2 1 2006
INSTITUTIONAL REVIEW BOARD
THE UNIVERSITY OF AKRON

THE FORMAT OF TRIANDIS BEHAVIORAL DIFFERENTIAL SCALE

A black ghetto dweller who is a communist

I would ____!____!____!____!____!____!____!____!____ would not
     admire the ideas of this person

I would ____!____!____!____!____!____!____!____!____ would not
     admire the character of this person

· I would ____!____!____!____!____!____!____!____!____ would not
     ask for the opinion of this person

I would ____!____!____!____!____!____!____!____!____ would not
     learn with the help of this person

I would ____!____!____!____!____!____!____!____!____ would not
     marry this person

I would ____!____!____!____!____!____!____!____!____ would not
     fall in love with this person

I would ____!____!____!____!____!____!____!____!____ would not
     go on a date with this person

I would ____!____!____!____!____!____!____!____!____ would not
     make love to this person

I would ____!____!____!____!____!____!____!____!____!____ would not
       be partners in athletic game with this person

I would ____!____!____!____!____!____!____!____!____!____ would not
       eat with this person

I would ____!____!____!____!____!____!____!____!____!____ would not
       gossip with this person

I would ____!____!____!____!____!____!____!____!____!____ would not
       accept this person as intimate friend

I would ____!____!____!____!____!____!____!____!____!____ would not
       exclude this person from my neighborhood

I would ____!____!____!____!____!____!____!____!____!____ would not
       prohibit this person from voting

I would ____!____!____!____!____!____!____!____!____!____ would not
       accept this person as a close kin by marriage

I would ____!____!____!____!____!____!____!____!____!____ would not
       invite this person to my club

I would ____!____!____!____!____!____!____!____!____!____ would not
       treat this person as a subordinate

I would ____!____!____!____!____!____!____!____!____!____ would not
       command this person

I would ____!____!____!____!____!____!____!____!____!____ would not
       obey this person

I would ____!____!____!____!____!____!____!____!____!____ would not
       criticize the work of this person

Source: Trandis (1971). Attitude and Attitude Change. Page 53

APPENDIX F

QUESTIONNAIRE DEVELOPMENT MATRIX

Items depicting Attitude/Behavior	Operational Definitions	References
I would/would not admire her ideas	Admiring or not admiring a person's idea stems from personal misgivings on the part of the actor about the credibility of the person of interest. Holding a person in high esteem makes her/his ideas admirable. Forming a poor image of a person makes her/his ideas worthless and non-admirable.	Blumer, (1937), etc.
I am/I am no comfortable taking directives from her	*A man who feels uncomfortable taking orders from a woman supervisor is likely suffering from some inferiority complex or feels his authority as a man is being challenged to disrepute either because he sees her as an underdog wielding power unconventionally.*	*Skrla, Reyes, & Scheurich, (2000)*

Items depicting Attitude/Behavior	Operational Definitions	References
I would/would not admire her character	Admiring a person's character is according that person some recognition, respect, and credit for qualities that that person possesses and exhibits	Triandis, (1971) Oduro & Macbeath, (2003)
I would/I would not vote her into a political office	Giving a person a-no-vote is declaring one's outright rejection of that person's competence to assume leadership position. In a sense, it connotes the denial of the candidate's ability to lead.	Mostafa, (2005)
I would/I would not gossip with her	Normally people gossip with people who share their opinions and beliefs; people they can identify with and feel comfortable in their presence; a person they can trust. Declaring one's intention not to gossip with her suggests distrust, not seeing the person as an equal to identify with or not a friend to be trusted.	Jalava, (2003)
I would/I would not accept her as an intimate friend	An inkling of some aversion being expressed here. If you cannot accept a person as an intimate friend then you have, at least some hidden discriminatory tendencies towards that person. There is no room for a common ground for social affinity here.	Ofie-Aboagye, (1994); Osmond & Thorn, (1993); Sugarman & Frankel, (1987)
I would/I would not support her promotion	You must have faith in and appreciation for a person's performance to support his/her promotion. Not willing to do so suggests two things: Lack of confidence in the person's ability and or some arbitrary dislike for that individual.	Bogardus, (1959)

Items depicting Attitude/Behavior	Operational Definitions	References
I would/I would not confide my secrets in her	This again suggests a lack of trust and disrespect for the person's integrity.	Blunner, (1937); Triandis & Gelfand, (1998)
I would/ would not defend her rights if they were jeopardized	Refusal to protect a person from being hurt physically or emotionally is an act of hatred or dislike for that person. It is a callous indifference to abuses to that person, mostly done out of hatred.	Triandis & Triandis, (1988)
I would/would not have her as my mentor	Acceptance of a person as one's mentor is an endorsement of the person's capabilities and abilities to mentor. A rejection of a person's mentorship may indicate a doubt on the part of the to-be-mentored of that person's ability or capabilities to be a mentor. It may also be indicative of personal dislike for the mentor-to-be due to some discriminatory tendencies.	Jalava, (2003): Buchan& Croson, (2004)

INSTRUMENT EVALUATION MATRIX (IEM) WITH INSTRUCTION FOR THE EXPERTS/JUDGES

For my internship project, I have constructed an instrument that will be used in measuring social distance. You are kindly requested to study and critique this ten-item Social Distance Scale (SDS), which is a hybrid of Bogardus' (1959) developed *Behavioral Differential Scale*. This scale is one of the instruments to be used in collecting data for my doctoral dissertation. The GSBDS scale measures the **attitude** of teachers towards **female principals** in some selected Ghanaian second cycle institutions.

The dissertation is a study that investigates the relationship between **gender ideological beliefs** of teachers (measured by SRES), and **teachers' attitudes** towards female principals (measured by GSBDS) of a representative sample of teachers from second cycle institutions in Ghana. The predictor and criterion variables to be measured in this study include **gender ideological** beliefs of teachers in the two Ghanaian lineage systems (patrilineal and matrilineal societies) and the **attitude of these teachers** towards their female principals respectfully.

Teachers may express the **traditional view** of gender ideology or the **egalitarian view** of gender ideology even in their attitudes towards their out-group (female principals). The researcher is interested in knowing to what extent can the content validity of the items on this instrument be established as measuring attitude or behavioral disposition depicting social distance? How is this scale a true measure of teachers' attitude? In other words, compared to traditional social distance scales, how truly representative is this instrument of known-measures of attitude when assessed behaviorally? Your comments and suggestions will be very helpful in the final development of a true and valid scale of measure for the teacher attitude variable

Gender discrimination is identified as a major social canker in the Ghanaian society (Ofei Aboagye, 1994; Oheneba-Sakyi, 1999; Awumbila, 2001; Akpalu 2001; and Chao, 1999).

As the Ghanaian society develops within the cultural defines of westernization, educational liberalism makes it possible for some women to break the myth about culturally supported male hegemony to assume leadership positions such as school principals. Being a patriarchal society, the Ghanaian culture favors a gender inequality that limits the status of women to subservient positions -- whether in the traditional or corporate sectors – and sees men as automatic authority figures. How well received female bosses are by their subordinates in the midst of the culturally supported male hegemony of the Ghanaian society is one of the concerns of this study. Discriminatory tendencies in a person can cloud the objective feelings towards and assessment of that individual's object of resentment. Consequently, not anyone who views females as subordinates of their male counterparts is likely to recognize or accept their leadership potentials and the authority positions they occupy.

Now, pretend as though you were one of the respondents (a teacher in Ghana). See if the statements make sense to you; whether the individual items will evoke genuine responses from respondents; any alterations needed? Do you agree or disagree with the formulation and structure of the items? Do you think the items look good the way they stand now? Your comments will be very helpful. First, study the questionnaire development matrix to understand the role of each item on the scale and let that guide you in your evaluation of the scale itself.

	Operational Definition	DOES THIS ITEM MEASURE WHAT IT IS INTENDED TO MEASURE- -SOCIAL DISTANCE?
		Put a "Check" in the boxes below if you think the item measures the concept (social distance) or "X" if you don't agree that the item is a good measure of social distance.
I would:___:___:___:___:___:___: I would not admire her ideas	Admiration for something or a person suggests a disposition to relate or start acquaintance with that thing or person. Not admiring a thing or person suggests non acquaintance.	
I am:___:___:___:___:___: I am not comfortable taking directives from her	A man who feels uncomfortable taking orders from a woman supervisor is likely suffering from some inferiority complex or feels his authority as a man is being challenged to disrepute; either because he sees her as an underdog wielding power unconventionally.	
I would:__:__:__:__:__:__: I would not admire her character	Admiring someone's character is the bases for building trust in that person.	
I would:___:___:___:___:___:___: I would not vote her into a political office	Entrusting someone with serious public office is indicative of some confidence in that person's ability and competency in authority to hold that office.	

I would:___:___:___:___:___:___: I would not gossip with her	Gossips are usually traded with people of trust; who can handle and treat confidentiality maturely.	
I would:___:___:___:___:___:___: I would not support her promotion	Supporting a person's promotion is indicative of some confidence in that person's ability and competency in authority to hold that office.	
I would:___:___:___:___:___:___: I would not accept as an intimate friend	Accepting a person as an intimate friend indicates finding some common grounds for a relationship with that person and also the readiness to treat that person as an equal.	
I would:___:___:___:___:___:___: I would not confide my secrets in her	Confiding one's secrets in a person indicates an absolute trust and respect in that person; a healthy ground for starting a relationship	
I would:__:___:___:___:___:___: I would not defend her rights if they were jeopardized	Standing up for somebody indicates some willingness to do self sacrifice on a person's part to and the conviction that the person deserves that gift of sacrifice and the support of the person defending her/his right if the were ever jeopardized.	
I would:___:___:___:___:___:___: I would not have her as my mentor	You reject a person's mentorship if you doubt the person's capabilities to be your mentor or if you do not trust the person's competence to be your mentor; or if you do not like that person or do not want her/him to be around you.	

APPENDIX H

CONGRUENCY TABLE ESTIMATING CONTENT VALIDITY

	Items Social Distance Items	Expert 1 -- 5 Expert-Judges Evaluations					
		Expert 1	Expert 2	Expert 3	Expert 4	Expert 5	%
1	I would/I would not admire her ideas	1	1	1	1	1	100%
2	I am/I am not comfortable taking directives from her	1	1	1	1	1	100%
3	I would/I would not admire her character	1	1	1	1	1	100%
4	I would/I would not vote her into a political office	1	1	1	1	1	100%
5	I would/I would not gossip with her	0	1	0	1	1	60%
6	I would/I would not accept her as an intimate friend	1	1	1	1	1	100%
7	I would/I would not support her promotion	1	1	1	1	1	100%
8	I would/I would not confide my secrets in her	1	1	0	1	1	80%
9	I would/I would not defend her rights if they were jeopardized	0	1	1	1	1	80%

10	I would/would not have as my mentor	1	1	1	1	1	100%
	Total Number of Affirmative Answers	8	10	7	10	10	45/50
	Percentage Scores	80%	100%	80%	100%	100%	
	Total Average Congruency Percentage Score (ACP)						**92%**

Note. The table illustrates their vetting. The check marks and the crosses indicating affirmation and rejection of items' validity were recoded for easy computation of scores. The checks were coded as "1" indicating affirmation and the crosses were coded as "0" indicating rejection.

APPENDIX I

PCA FACTOR ANALYSIS

Table I1. *SPSS PCA table of factor loadings of the eigenvalues and total variance explained*

	Initial Eigenvalues			Rotation Sums of Squared Loadings		
Component	Total	% of Variance	Cumulative %	Total	% of Variance	Cumulative %
1	4.565	45.653	45.653	3.874	38.740	38.740
2	1.534	15.340	60.993	2.225	22.253	60.993
3	.820	8.203	69.196			
4	.636	6.360	75.556			
5	.588	5.877	81.433			
6	.494	4.941	86.374			
7	.387	3.867	90.241			
8	.366	3.659	93.900			
9	.314	3.136	97.036			
10	.296	2.964	100.000			

Note. Extraction Method: Principal Component Analysis. *Factors 1 and 2 ˃ 1.*

Table 12. *Component matrix for accommodative disposition sub-scale*

Items	Component
	1
1-I would/would not admire her ideas	.821
2-I am/am not comfortable taking orders from her	.820
3-I would/would not admire her character	.772
9-I would/would not defend her rights if they were jeopardized	.747
7-I would/would not support her promotion	.724,
10-I would/would not have her as my mentor	.666

Note. Extraction Method: Principal Component Analysis
Rotation Method: Varimax with Kaiser Normalization

Table 13. *Component matrix for inter personal affective disposition sub-scale*

Items	Component
	2
6-I would/would not accept as an intimate friend	.812
8-I would/would not confide my secrets in her	.783
4-I would/would not vote her into a political office	.647

Note. Extraction Method: PrincipalComponent Analysis
Rotation Method: Varimax with Kaiser Normalization

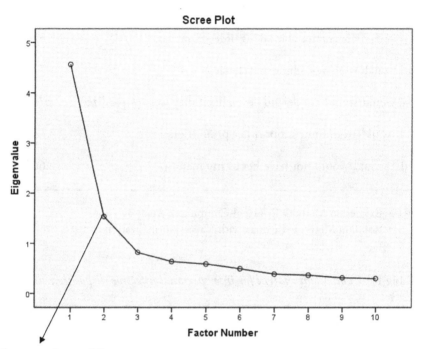

Trajectory Point of Disjunction

Figure I1. Scree plot showing 2 factors on the GSBDS scale

Note. Scree Plot on a bicoordinate plane showing the Eigenvalues that are greater than 1 indicated by the trajectory point of disjunction.

Rotated Factor Matrix
1

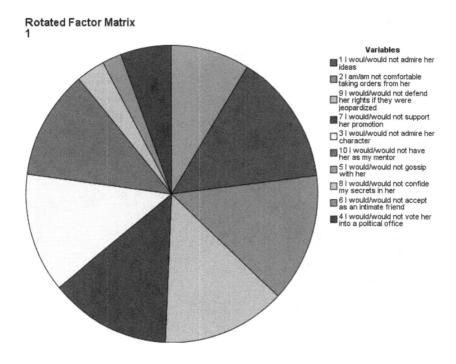

Figure 12. A pie chart showing orthogonal loadings of all the items eigenvalues when rotated

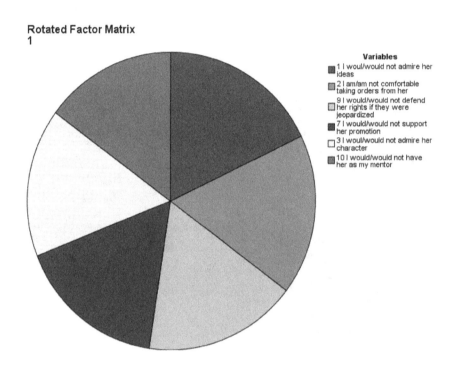

Figure 13. A pie chart showing eigenvalues loadings of 6 items on the GSBDS (items 1, 2, 3, 7, 9, & 10) on Factor 1

Rotated Factor Matrix 2

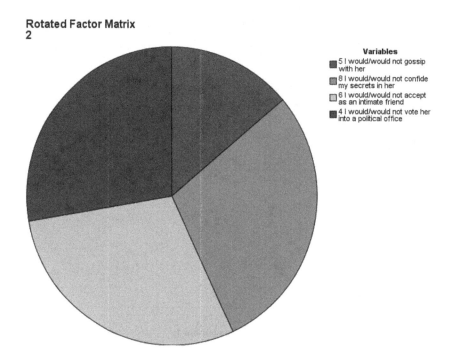

Variables
- 5 I would/would not gossip with her
- 8 I would/would not confide my secrets in her
- 6 I would/would not accept as an intimate friend
- 4 I would/would not vote her into a political office

Figure 14. A pie chart showing 4 items (4, 5, 6, and 8) that loaded on Factor 2

Note. Item 5 was dropped for cross-loading

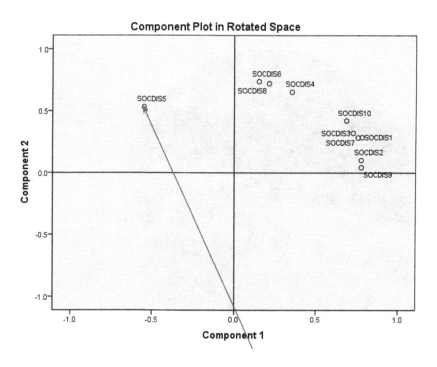

Figure I5. Factor plot in rotated space showing item 5 having no important value on any of the factors.

APPENDIX J

RELIABILITY TABLES FOR DVs

Table J1. *Cronbach's alpha reliability coefficient for accommodative disposition sub-scale*

Cronbach's Alpha	Cronbach's Alpha Based on Standardized Items	N of Items
.883	.885	6

Table J2. *Cronbach's alpha reliability coefficient for inter personal affective disposition sub-scale*

Cronbach's Alpha	Cronbach's Alpha Based on Standardized Items	N of Items
.682	.683	3

APPENDIX K

MULTICOLLINEARITY TABLES

Table K1. *Correlations among the predictors of the study to detect the presence of Multicollinearity*

	Respondent's Lineage Ties	Respondent's Age	Respondent's Gender	Degree of Egalitarianism
Respondent's Lineage Ties	-			
Respondent's Age	-.017	-		
Respondent's Gender	.064	.043	-	
Degree of Egalitarianism	.024	.159**	.067	-

**Correlation is significant at the 0.01 level (2-tailed).

Table K2 . *Coefficients output for INTADISPO showing the VIF for all X variables*

Model	Unstandardized Coefficients		Standardized Coefficients			Collinearity Statistics	
	B	Std. Error	Beta	t	Sig	Tolerance	VIF
(Constant)	12.999	3.233	4.021	.000			
Respondent's Lineage Ties	.216	.448	.027	.483	.629	.995	1.005
Respondent's Gender	.293	.451	.037	.650	.516	.991	1.009
Respondent's Age	-2.034	1.820	-.064	-1.117	.265	.970	1.031
Degree of Egalitarianism	.002	.006	.023	.393	.695	.966	1.035

Note. Dependent variable: Interpersonal Affective Disposition Domain (Intadispo); Regression Coefficients Within Normal Range

Table K3. *Coefficients output for ACCODISPO showing the VIF for all X variables*

Model	Unstandardized Coefficients		Standardized Coefficients			Collinearity Statistics	
	B	Std. Error	Beta	t	Sig	Tolerance	VIF
1 (Constant)	12.999	3.233		4.021	.000		
Respondent's Lineage Ties	.216	.448	.027	.483	.629	.995	1.005
Respondent's Gender	.293	.451	.037	.650	.516	.991	1.009
TransAge	-2.034	1.820	-.064	-1.117	.265	.970	1.031
Degree of Egalitarianism	.002	.006	.023	.393	.695	.966	1.035

Note. Dependent Variable: Accommodative Disposition Domain (ACCODISPO); Regression coefficients within normal range

APPENDIX L

TABLES AND FIGURES FOR NORMALITY AND MULTIVARIATE OUTLIERS

Table L1. *Mahalanobis distance test for ACCODISPO*

| | Residuals Statistics[a] | | | | |
	Min.	Max.	Mean	Std. Deviation	N
Predicted Value	9.5327	23.4393	16.1561	2.68682	314
Std. Predicted Value	-2.465	2.711	.000	1.000	314
SE of Predicted Value	.606	1.503	.828	.137	314
Ad. Predicted Value	9.4944	23.2290	16.1529	2.69122	314
Residual	-14.88748	17.42387	.00000	6.60569	314
Std. Residual	-2.239	2.621	.000	.994	314
Stud. Residual	-2.260	2.645	.000	1.002	314
Deleted Residual	-15.16344	17.74416	.00318	6.71277	314
Stud. Deleted Residual	-2.275	2.671	.001	1.004	314
Mahal. Distance	1.605	15.010	3.987	1.740	314
Cook's Distance	.000	.032	.003	.004	314
Centered Leverage Value	.005	.048	.013	.006	314

Note. ACCODISPO = Accommodative Disposition Scale; Mahalanobis Distance Score of 15.010 indicating no multivariate outliers with 18.47 critical value

Table L2. *Shapiro-Wilk tests of normality for gender and lineage ties by the continuous variables of the study*

	Kolmogorov-Smirnov[a]			Shapiro-Wilk		
	Statistic	df	Sig.	Statistic	df	Sig.
By Gender						
Respondent's Age						
Male	.088	174	.002	.961	174	.000
Female	.114	140	.000	.953	140	.000
Accodispo						
Male	.130	174	.000	.926	174	.000
Female	.079	140	.033	.961	140	.000
Intadispo						
Male	.084	174	.005	.971	174	.001
Female	.098	140	.002	.971	140	.005
Degree of Egalitarianism						
Male	.063	174	.093	.986	174	.081
Female	.086	140	.014	.978	140	.026
By Lineage Tie						
Respondent's Age						
Patrlineal	.076	166	.021	.974	166	.003
Matrilineal	.117	148	.000	.949	148	.000
Accodispo						
Patrlineal	.113	166	.000	.938	166	.000
Matrilineal	.090	148	.005	.947	148	.000
Intadispo						
Patrlineal	.083	166	.007	.978	166	.009
Matrilineal	.114	148	.000	.963	148	.001
Degree of Egalitarianism						
Patrlineal	.059	166	.200*	.986	166	.100
Matrilineal	.084	148	.012	.976	148	.011

Note. ACCODISPO = Accommodative disposition; INTADISPO = Interpersonal affective disposition; * This is a lower bound of the true significance; a. Lilliefors Significance Correction

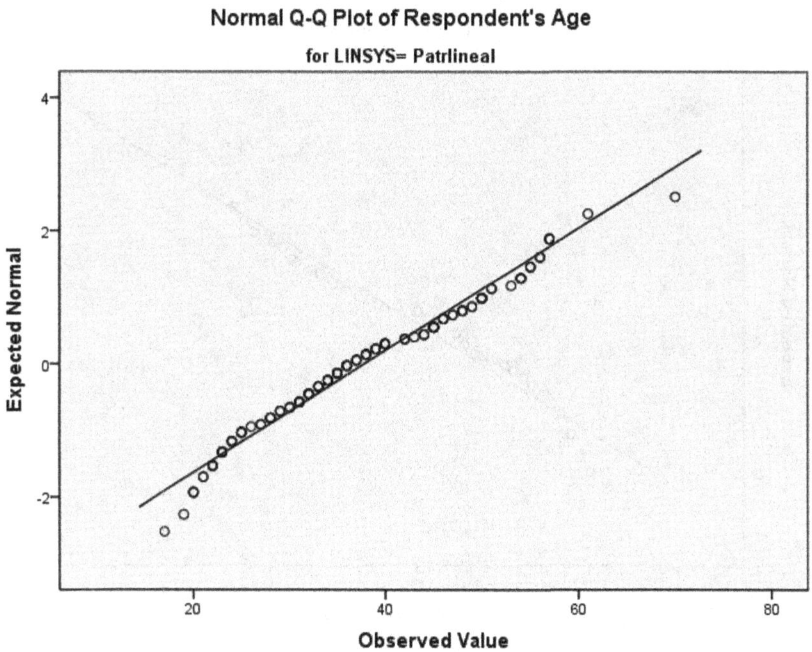
Normal Q-Q Plot of Respondent's Age
for LINSYS= Patrlineal
Expected Normal
4
2
0
-2
20
40
60
80
Observed Value

Figure L1. Q-Q plot showing outliers in the distribution of scores for age by lineage ties

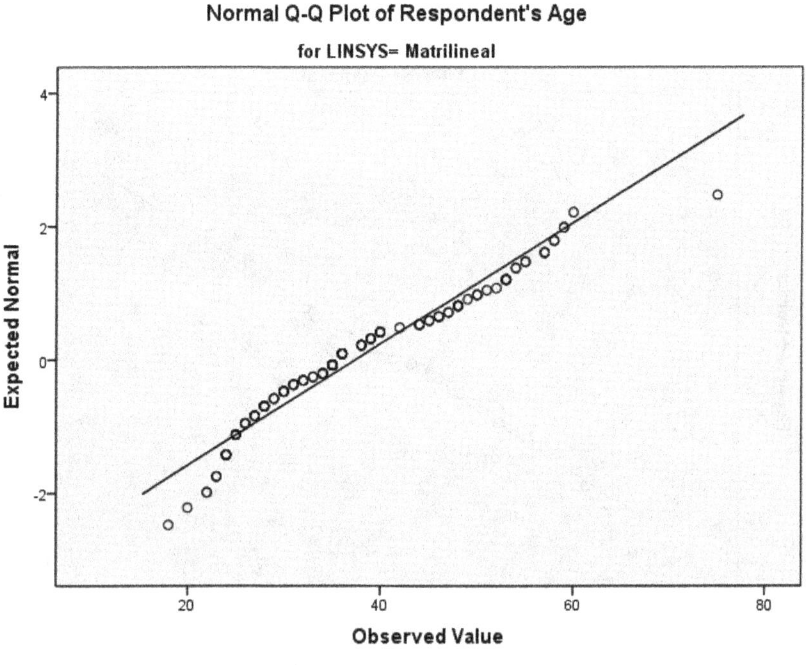
Normal Q-Q Plot of Respondent's Age
for LINSYS= Matrilineal
Expected Normal
Observed Value
4
2
0
-2
20
40
60
80

Figure L2. Q-Q plot showing outliers in the distribution of scores for age by lineage ties

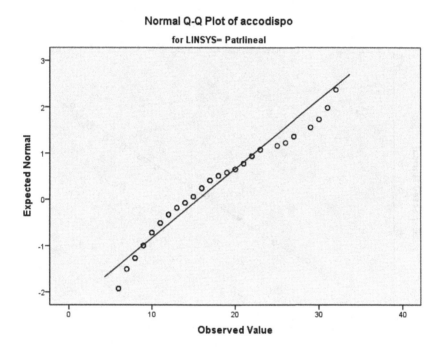

Figure L3. Q-Q plot showing outliers in the distribution of scores for ACCODISPO by lineage ties

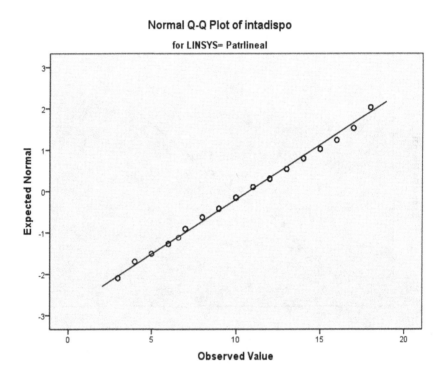

Figure L4 . Q-Q plot showing no outliers in the distribution of scores for INTADISPO by lineage ties

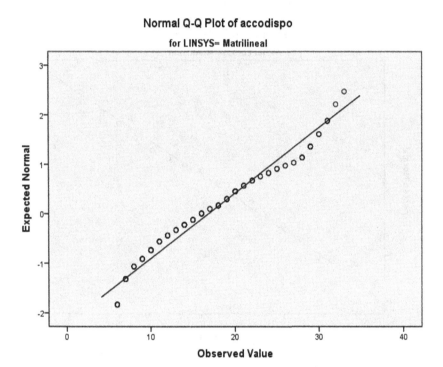

Figure L5. Q-Q plot showing outliers in the distribution of scores for ACCODISPO by lineage ties

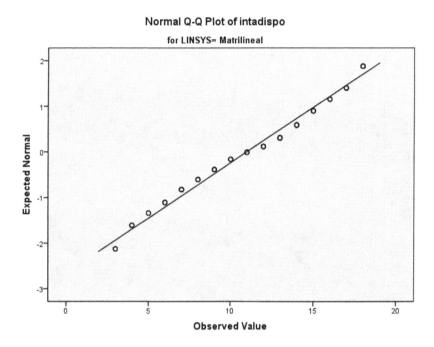

Figure L6. Q-Q plot showing no outliers in the distribution of scores for INTADISPO by lineage ties

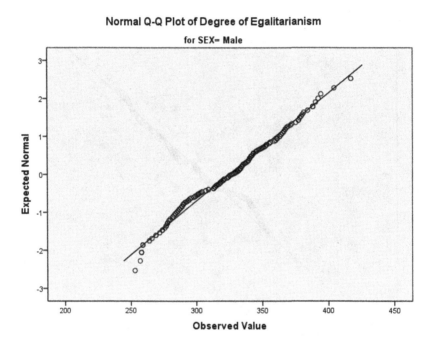

Figure L7. Q-Q plot showing no outliers in the distribution of scores for egalitarianism by gender

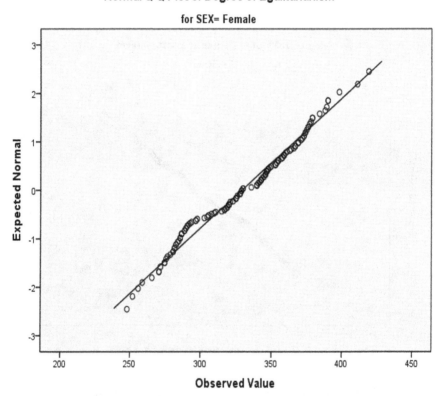

Figure L8. Q-Q plot showing no outliers in the distribution of scores for egalitarianism by gender

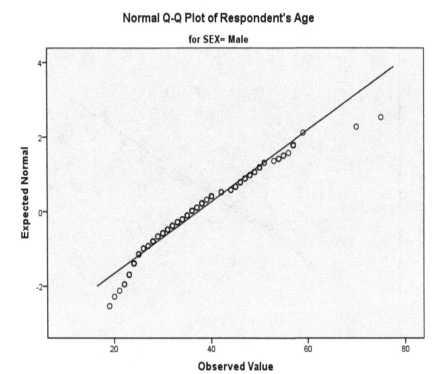

Figure L9. Q-Q plot showing outliers in the distribution of scores for age by gender

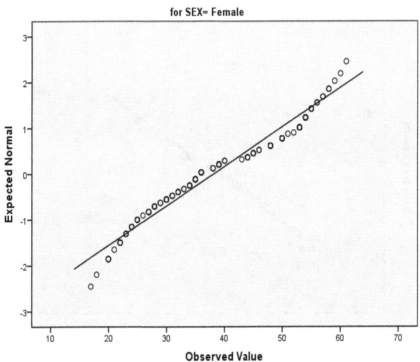

Figure L10. Q-Q plot showing outliers in the distribution of scores for age by gender

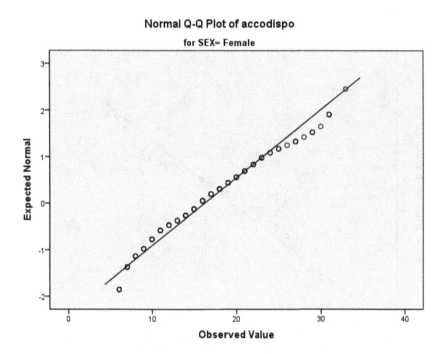

Figure L11. Q-Q plot showing outliers in the distribution of scores for ACCODISPO by gender

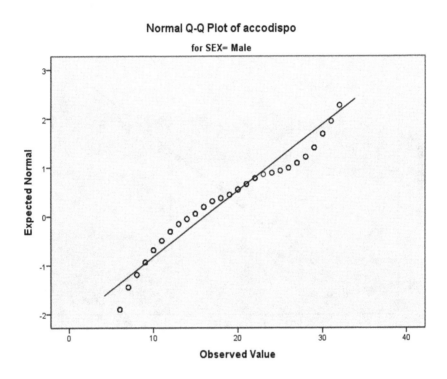

Figure L12. Q-Q plot showing outliers in the distribution of scores for ACCODISPO by gender

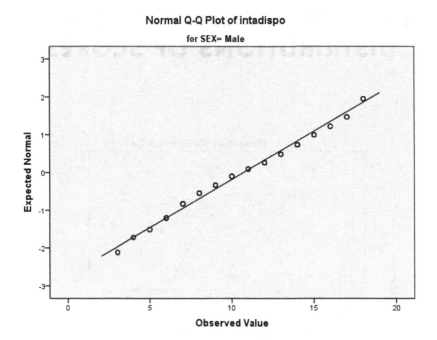

Figure L13. Q-Q plot showing no outliers in the distribution of scores for INTADISPO by gender

APPENDIX M

FIGURES SHOWING NORMAL DISTRIBUTIONS OF SCORES

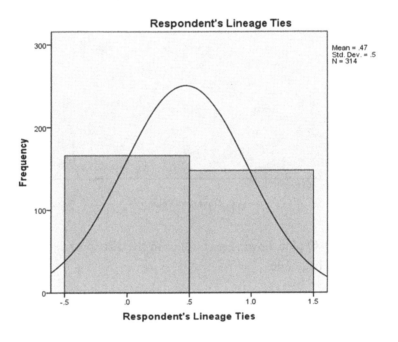

Figure M1. Normal curve for respondent's lineage ties variable

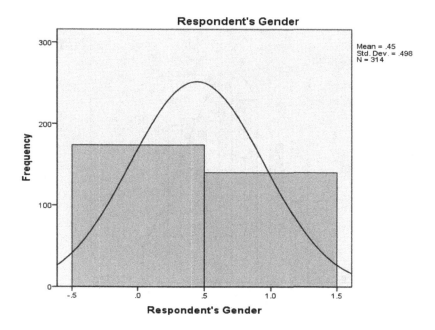

Figure M2. Normal curve for respondent's gender variable

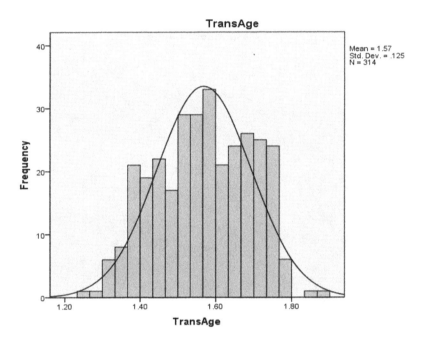

Figure M3. Normal curve for respondent's age variable

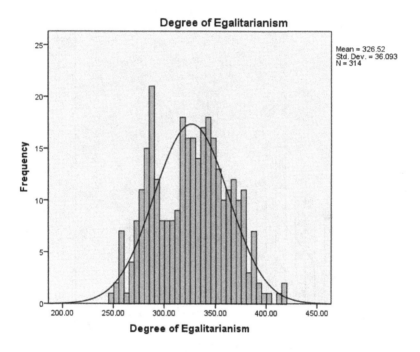

Figure M4. Normal curve for degree of egalitarianism variable

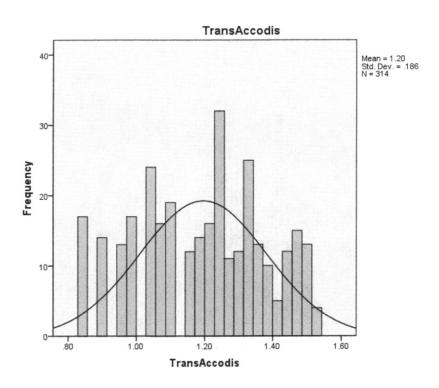

Figure M5. Normal curve for accommodative disposition domain

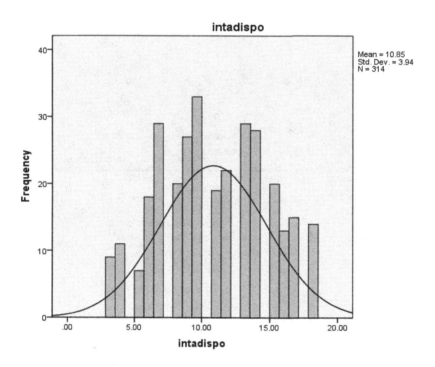

Figure M6. Normal curve for interpersonal affective disposition domain

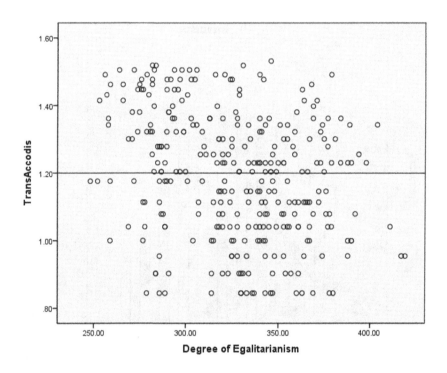

Figure M7. Scatterplot of predicted values of ACCODISPO by degree of egalitarianism; residuals, showing assumptions met

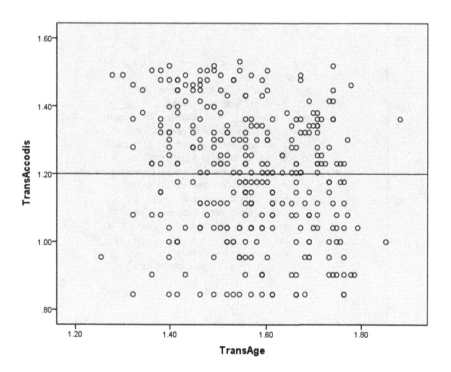

Figure M8. Scatterplot of predicted values of ACCODISPO by age against residuals, showing assumptions met

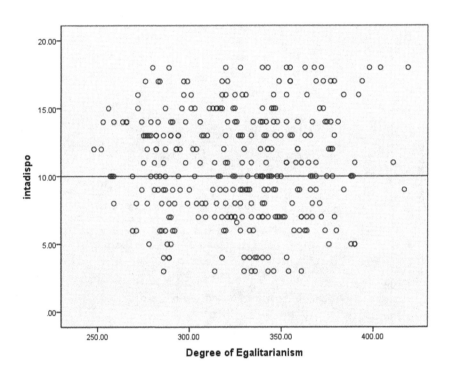

Figure M9. Scatterplot of predicted values of INTADISPO degree of egalitarianism against residuals, showing assumptions met

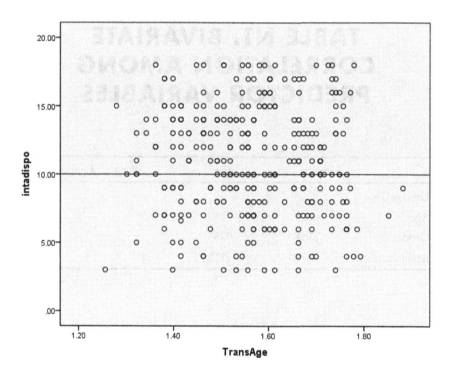

Figure M10. Scatterplot of predicted values of INTADISPO against residuals, showing assumptions met

APPENDIX N

TABLE N1. BIVARIATE CORRELATION AMONG PREDICTOR VARIABLES

	Lineage Ties	Age	Gender	Egalitarianism
Lineage Ties	-			
Age	-.015	-		
Gender	.064	.025	-	
Egalitarianism	.024	.171**	.067	-

Table N2. *Mean, Standard Deviations, and Intercorrelations (Pearson R) for Interpersonal Affective Disposition Domain and Predictors*

	M	SD	1	2	3	4
[a]Interpersonal affective disposition			.031	.039	-.060	.015
1. Lineage Tie	-	.500	-	.064	-.015	.024
2. Gender	-	.498		-	.025	.067
3. Age[a]	1.569	.125			-	.171**
4. Egalitarianism[a]	326.519	36.093				-

Note. **. Correlation is significant at the 0.01 level (2-tailed); [$p > .05$];
[a]Transformed variables.

Table N3. *Mean, Standard Deviations, and Intercorrelations (Pearson R) for Accommodative Disposition Domain and Predictors*

	M	SD	1	2	3	4
Accommodative disposition[a]	1.196	.186	.066	.023	-.202**	-.299**
Predictors						
1. Lineage Tie	-	.500	-	.064	-.015	.024
2. Gender	-	.498		-	.025	.067
3. Age[a]	1.569	.125			-	.171**
4. Egalitarianism[a]	326.519	36.093				-

Note. **Correlation is significant at the 0.01 level (2-tailed); [$p < .001$]; [a]Transformed variables.

APPENDIX O

AFRICA MAP SHOWING GHANA IN SUB-SAHARAN AFRICA

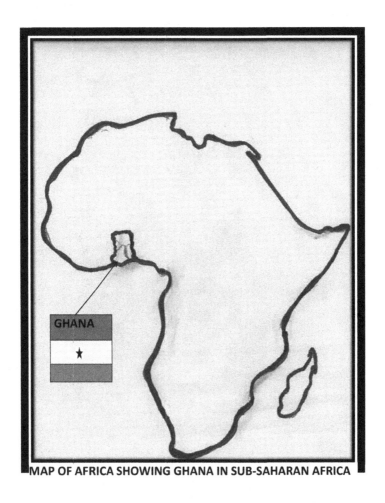

MAP OF AFRICA SHOWING GHANA IN SUB-SAHARAN AFRICA